T0100901

Praise for *Bold Pursuit*

"If you are looking for a book that will teach you proper theology and sound doctrine, challenge you spiritually, refute false teachings, sharpen your discernment, and give you practical tips on how to live the victorious Christian life, *Bold Pursuit* is the perfect ninety-day devotional that leads you into a more intimate relationship with God. Purchase one book for yourself, and then purchase another and give it to a friend. This is a must-read for any Christian serious about growing in their walk with God."

—ALLEN PARR, AUTHOR OF *MISLED* AND FOUNDER
OF THE BEAT YOUTUBE CHANNEL

"I am glad Daniel wrote *Bold Pursuit*, which covers the basics of being a follower of Jesus. It took me the better part of forty years before I realized that spiritual growth is understanding the basic principles and truths in a deeper way. This excites me because the book in your hands will cover the basics—deeper and deeper. If you reread it ten years from now, you will ask yourself, 'How did I miss this or that when I read it the first time?' Reading it will make you a better and more godly man. *Bold Pursuit* will lead men to be men with principles, strong in the Word, and living in the fire of holiness. Such men will say to the world, 'Come, this is the path we need to take. This is the way to live.'"

—BENNIE MOSTERT, WRITER, PRAYER MOBILIZER, AND DISCIPLE-MAKER

BOLD PURSUIT

A 90-Day Devotional for Men

Seeking the Heart of God

DANIEL MARITZ

NELSON
BOOKS

An Imprint of Thomas Nelson

Bold Pursuit

© 2023 by Daniel Maritz

Published in Nashville, Tennessee, by Nelson Books, an imprint of Thomas Nelson. Nelson Books and Thomas Nelson are registered trademarks of HarperCollins Christian Publishing, Inc.

Thomas Nelson titles may be purchased in bulk for educational, business, fundraising, or sales promotional use. For information, please email SpecialMarkets@ThomasNelson.com.

Scripture quotations are taken from the New American Standard Bible® (NASB). Copyright © 1960, 1962, 1963, 1968, 1971, 1972, 1973, 1975, 1977, 1995, 2020 by The Lockman Foundation. Used by permission. www.lockman.org

Any internet addresses, phone numbers, or company or product information printed in this book are offered as a resource and are not intended in any way to be or to imply an endorsement by Thomas Nelson, nor does Thomas Nelson vouch for the existence, content, or services of these sites, phone numbers, companies, or products beyond the life of this book.

ISBN 978-1-4002-4297-9 (eBook)
ISBN 978-1-4002-4296-2 (HC)

Library of Congress Control Number: 2023937552

Printed in the United States of America

23 24 25 26 27 LBC 5 4 3 2 1

I want to dedicate this book, written specifically for men,
to the best man I ever knew.
The man who taught me about the wonderful truths of God.
The man who lived the way he preached.
The man who was my role model.
The man whom God chose to be my earthly father,
Etienne Maritz.

Contents

Introduction

DAVID ASKED GOD TO "CREATE IN ME A CLEAN HEART,
God, and renew a steadfast spirit within me" (Psalm 51:10). One of the
most famous men in the Bible, who had an unbelievable relationship
with God, was David. He was a man after God's own heart.

How many men who call themselves Christians can say that
today?
How many men ask God the same request that David asked?
How many men are really serious about their relationship
with God?
How many men know God intimately?

I believe all of us men should have this burning desire to have a
deep relationship with God the way David did. David walked closely
with God and we still learn from his life today, thousands of years
later. He had an unstoppable desire to know the God of all creation
intimately, not just know about Him. This ninety-day devotional was
created to help us to deeply know God. Each devotional is a guide to
grow closer to God and learn what it means to truly abide in Christ.

I believe thousands of "Christian" men today are lukewarm,
and they do not realize that God will spit them out of His mouth!
There's a big problem in the church today, a problem of lukewarm
men who care more about living for the things of this world than
about living for the God of this world. The gospel messages we hear
in many churches across the globe are often sensational, superficial,
and materialistic. We hear a watered-down gospel aimed at tickling
ears instead of transforming lives and saving souls for Christ.

I wrote this book to cut through all the noise and bring back
the sound doctrine of Scripture. I want to do so in truth and love,

pointing men across the world to pick up their cross and follow Jesus, to respect Him, to understand His holiness, to seek Him and His righteousness first in everything they do.

Bold Pursuit calls us to radical discipleship, which can only come from wholehearted devotion to Jesus Christ. I will turn to the Bible and teach spiritual truths that will help us understand what it means to truly abide in Christ and to fully surrender to His will for our lives. This is what we need in the church today.

You cannot serve Christ with only your heart or only your mind; you need both. In other words, you need to follow Christ with the right doctrine and devotion. You also need to know what it means to follow Christ in the Spirit and not in the flesh. God has called me to share the good news to the ends of the world, to all people and all nations, to teach the Word in season and out of season, and to show people what it means to be a reborn Christian.

My heart for this book is that men around the world will come to understand that the God of the past is the same God of the present and the future. We can have a relationship with Him like David had. We can read and study His unchanging truth in the Bible in the same way godly men did—men like John Wesley, Charles Spurgeon, Jonathan Edwards, D. L. Moody, Billy Graham, Andrew Murray, and my father, Etienne Maritz, here in South Africa.

Bold Pursuit will challenge us to look in the mirror to examine whether we are in the faith and whether we follow Christ with our whole heart, mind, and soul. This book will require a new and fresh commitment to God and a burning desire to please Him in all that we do. Most of us do not realize that God is more eager to love us and answer our prayers than we are to love Him and pray to Him.

God is always waiting—the God of the universe is always there waiting for us. God is more eager to reveal Himself to us than we are to seek Him. It's time we turned back to God fully, it's time we fall on our knees, and it's time we return to the Bible. This devotional will guide you to do just that.

Before you start with the first daily devotional, pray that God will bless you and reveal Himself to you as you continue to work through the ninety days. Read and work through each entry with your Bible every day, making it a daily routine. There will be a few questions at the end of every devotional, and I want you to answer them honestly and keep a notebook close by to write down important notes that you feel God wants you to focus on.

Finally, be humble and open so that God can change you according to His will. He is the potter and you are the clay.

No Matter the Cost

Fight the good fight of faith.
—1 TIMOTHY 6:12

LIFE IS SHORT, AND EACH OF US MUST DECIDE HOW WE will spend our time. The apostle Paul said, "So then, be careful how you walk, not as unwise people but as wise, making the most of your time, because the days are evil. Therefore do not be foolish, but understand what the will of the Lord is" (Ephesians 5:15–17).

The devil is relentless in his efforts to undermine God's work and advance evil. God's will is for us to take a stand, to push back against the darkness. Paul said, "Be on the alert, stand firm in the faith, act like men, be strong" (1 Corinthians 16:13). That bravery and strength can take many different forms.

It is crucial that we fight through the Spirit, not the flesh. Fighting through the flesh gives power to the Enemy. Even when we fight in the name of God, if we fight through the flesh, we will do more harm than good. Only the Spirit can help us fight the right battles effectively.

Most of the apostles and early Christian leaders were put to death because of their faith. Paul was beheaded. Peter was crucified. John escaped being killed but was held as a prisoner on the island of Patmos. We may never face martyrdom, torture, or imprisonment for our faith as the early Christians did, but our commitment to Christ should be no less radical than theirs. Jesus made it clear that there is no place in God's kingdom for lukewarm Christians. We cannot live for God and for the sinful world.

Jesus said, "If anyone wants to come after Me, he must deny himself, take up his cross, and follow Me. For whoever wants to save his life will lose it; but whoever loses his life for My sake will find it" (Matthew 16:24–25). If we truly follow Jesus Christ, we need to destroy our own selfish, sinful desires. We need to give our whole heart, our whole soul, and our whole mind to Jesus.

That's easier said than done in this immoral, materialistic world we live in, because our sinful nature wants to live in sin. That's why Jesus encouraged His followers to think in terms of investment: "For what good will it do a person if he gains the whole world, but forfeits his soul? Or what will a person give in exchange for his soul?" (Matthew 16:26). Success, popularity, comfort, and safety in this world may seem like valuable things to strive for, but they're all fleeting and ultimately worthless when our lives are over. Their value pales in comparison to the value of where our souls will be for all eternity.

This takes us back to where we started. This world is temporary, a drop in the ocean compared to the eternal life God has in store for us. If we invest ourselves in standing up for God's truth, no matter the cost, we will enjoy the rewards forever.

DIG DEEP

This is a call to action. As a reborn believer, you must engage in the fight against the devil and his forces. There's too much at stake to sit on the sidelines. Ask yourself the following questions and answer them truthfully:

1. What would a battle against evil influences look like in your life? Are you fully committed to God?
2. What is the difference between fighting in the flesh and fighting in the Spirit?
3. How does God equip you for battle?

Nothing but the Truth

Be diligent to present yourself approved to God
as a worker who does not need to be ashamed,
accurately handling the word of truth.
—2 TIMOTHY 2:15

CAN YOU THINK OF SOMETHING YOU LEARNED AS A CHILD that turned out to be untrue? Maybe you believed in Santa Claus. Or you were taught that eating carrots improves your vision. When you discovered the truth, you may have been a little embarrassed or annoyed. But in the big picture of your life, that knowledge probably didn't have much of an impact. When it comes to spiritual things, however, the stakes are much higher.

Since the beginning of Christianity, there have been false teachers. Jesus predicted them. The disciples battled them. Many early churches were nearly destroyed because of them. Peter said, "But false prophets also appeared among the people, just as there will also be false teachers among you, who will secretly introduce destructive heresies, even denying the Master who bought them, bringing swift destruction upon themselves" (2 Peter 2:1). False teachers still cause huge problems for believers today.

James 3:1 makes it clear that false teachers will be held accountable for their actions: "Do not become teachers in large numbers, my brothers, since you know that we who are teachers will incur a stricter judgment."

But here's something important for all reborn believers to understand: we, too, will be held accountable for the teachings we allow to take root in our lives. That's why it's important to make sure that we're constantly being challenged by God's truth, instead of settling for teachings that comfort us or make us feel good about ourselves. We need to change our lifestyle according to Scripture and never try to change the Bible according to our lifestyle. Paul said, "For the time will come when they will not endure sound doctrine; but wanting to have their ears tickled, they will accumulate for themselves teachers in accordance with their own desires" (2 Timothy 4:3).

God has given us everything we need in His Word to recognize false teachings. Paul said, "All Scripture is inspired by God and profitable for teaching, for reproof, for correction, for training in righteousness; so that the man or woman of God may be fully capable, equipped for every good work" (2 Timothy 3:16–17). Our job is to study Scripture so that we have a thorough understanding of the truth.

John said, "Beloved, do not believe every spirit, but test the spirits to see whether they are from God, because many false prophets have gone out into the world" (1 John 4:1). Testing every message we receive helps us recognize when someone is lying to us, telling us things we want to hear instead of things we need to hear. When we know the truth of Scripture, we won't be easily fooled by messages such as "God is happy with you just as you are" or "God wants you to be rich and comfortable."

God's Word is filled with life-changing truth. Why settle for empty lies?

DIG DEEP

Knowing the truth allows us to recognize teaching that has been changed or watered down. Ask yourself the following questions and answer them truthfully:

1. How might a false teaching take root in your life?
2. How do you recognize false teaching?

Words Matter

The one who desires life, to love and see good days, must
keep his tongue from evil and his lips from speaking deceit.
—1 PETER 3:10

THE TONGUE HAS THE POWER TO DESTROY. ONE MOMENT
of frustration or anger, one impulsive choice of words, or one
momentary lapse of judgment can change a person's life forever.
James warned, "And the tongue is a fire, the very world of unrighteousness; the tongue is set among our body's parts as that which
defiles the whole body and sets on fire the course of our life, and is
set on fire by hell" (James 3:6).

Yet we can also use our words in positive ways. First, *we can use*
our words to honor God's sacred name. "You shall not take the name of
the LORD your God in vain" (Exodus 20:7). God gives us the privilege
of using His name in our worship and prayer. Speaking it draws us
closer to Him. On the other hand, misusing His name puts distance
in our relationship with Him. We can show others what it means to
be a new creation by refusing to use OMG—or any variation of the
Lord's name—as a thoughtless expression.

Second, *we can refuse to talk about luck or superstition.* James said,
"Every good thing given and every perfect gift is from above, coming down from the Father of lights, with whom there is no variation
or shifting shadow" (James 1:17). Our blessings are not the result of
random chance or superstitious nonsense. We can help others see
that by giving God the credit for our blessings.

Third, *we can honor our word.* Jesus said, "The one who is faithful in a very little thing is also faithful in much; and the one who is unrighteous in a very little thing is also unrighteous in much" (Luke 16:10). If people know they can trust us to follow through on the little things, such as showing up when we say we're going to, they may begin to trust us with the big things. When our actions match our words, we can make a profound difference in someone's life.

Fourth, *we can build people up, instead of breaking them down.* "Let no unwholesome word come out of your mouth, but if there is any good word for edification according to the need of the moment, say that, so that it will give grace to those who hear" (Ephesians 4:29). Stay away from gossip. Never judge someone through your flesh, but if led by the Spirit, judge righteously to build others up in the faith.

Always remember to let your light shine, especially in difficult times, because that is what sets us apart from the world. People who do not know God will normally be anxious in times of trouble, but we trust God to work all things together for good if we put Him first in our lives. We live by faith and not by sight, and that truth always needs to guide the way we talk to other people.

DIG DEEP

Our words matter—all of them. Ask yourself the following questions and answer them truthfully:

1. What are the biggest challenges you face in trying to control your tongue?
2. How can you use your words to show others what it means to be a new creation in Christ?

Know Your Enemy

Be of sober spirit, be on the alert. Your adversary, the devil, prowls around like a roaring lion, seeking someone to devour.
—1 PETER 5:8

IF YOU'VE EVER PLAYED SPORTS, YOU KNOW THE IMPOR-tance of a scouting report. Knowing what an opponent is likely to do helps you prepare a successful game plan. In warfare, where the stakes are much higher, spies risk their lives to provide intelligence on an enemy's plans.

Peter gave reborn Christians a scouting report on our enemy in the passage above. Giving us key intelligence about Satan is one way God equips us for spiritual battle. Paul warned that Satan tries to take advantage of people. But then Paul said, "We are not ignorant of his schemes" (2 Corinthians 2:11).

Lying is the key to Satan's designs. Jesus said, "There is no truth in him," and He called Satan "the father of lies" (John 8:44). His lies can have a devastating impact on people's lives—now and forever. Satan "has blinded the minds of the unbelieving so that they will not see the light of the gospel of the glory of Christ, who is the image of God" (2 Corinthians 4:4). That's why it's important for believers to counter Satan's lies with the truth of the gospel.

Satan uses people, including those closest to us, to distract us from God's will. He even tried to do this with Jesus. When Jesus told His disciples that He would be killed and then raised from the dead on the third day, "Peter took Him aside and began to rebuke Him, saying, 'God forbid it, Lord! This shall never happen to You!' But He turned and said to Peter, 'Get behind Me, Satan! You are a stumbling block to Me; for you are not setting your mind on God's purposes, but men's'" (Matthew 16:22–23).

Satan sends demons to trouble us and steal our peace and joy. Paul wrote, "For our struggle is not against flesh and blood, but against the rulers, against the powers, against the world forces of this darkness, against the spiritual forces of wickedness in the heavenly places" (Ephesians 6:12).

Satan is a dangerous enemy, but he is no match for God. He is a created being. He can do only what God allows him to, as we see in the story of Job (Job 2:6). James gave us the secret to overcoming our powerful, but limited, enemy: "Submit therefore to God. Resist the devil and he will flee from you" (James 4:7).

God can use Satan's attacks to make us stronger and wiser, and bring us closer to Him. Paul said, "For I am convinced that neither death, nor life, nor angels, nor principalities, nor things present, nor things to come, nor powers, nor height, nor depth, nor any other created thing will be able to separate us from the love of God which is in Christ Jesus our Lord" (Romans 8:38–39). The more we resist the devil and his strategies, the closer we grow to God.

DIG DEEP

The more you resist Satan, the less influence he has over your life. Ask yourself the following questions and answer them truthfully:

1. What does resisting the devil look like in your life?
2. How might God use Satan's attacks to strengthen you and bring you closer to Him?

Put On the Belt of Truth

Stand firm therefore, having belted your waist with truth.
—EPHESIANS 6:14

THE MOMENT WE PLACE OUR FAITH IN CHRIST WE BECOME
His soldiers, enter the spiritual battlefield, and gain an enemy for
life—Satan, the fallen angel whose rebellion against God brought
evil into this world. Peter described Satan as a "roaring lion, seeking
someone to devour" (1 Peter 5:8).

But God does not leave us unprotected against this roaring,
devouring enemy. He gives us spiritual armor for our battle. Paul
said, "Put on the full armor of God, so that you will be able to stand
firm against the schemes of the devil" (Ephesians 6:11).

The first piece of this armor is the belt of truth. A belt is worn
close to the body. It surrounds us. Surrounding ourselves with truth
prepares us for battle with Satan, who constantly bombards us with
lies. He lies to us through false teachers, politicians, the media,
friends, and even family members. He also lies to us through our
own feelings. Satan even makes us question whether God really cares
for us. Without the truth, we're susceptible to his lies. When we put
on the belt of truth, we surround ourselves with God's promises and
commands. The more we know about them through studying His
Word, the more secure our armor will be.

One of the lies Satan uses is that following Christ and His commandments will trap us in a dull and miserable existence. The
opposite is true because we can never find true joy in this world; we
find joy in Jesus Christ (Psalm 16:11). By making people slaves to sin,

Satan distorts their perspective. But Jesus told His followers, "You will know the truth, and the truth will make you free" (John 8:32). By setting people free from sin, Jesus helps us see what true joy really is.

Paul said, "For the wrath of God is revealed from heaven against all ungodliness and unrighteousness of people who suppress the truth in unrighteousness" (Romans 1:18). Many unbelievers knowingly embrace lies because the truth is too hard to face. And they want others to join them in their lies so they can keep up their illusion. But reborn believers are called to speak "the truth in love" (Ephesians 4:15). Often that means shining a light on things that others prefer to keep hidden. People don't like that. And that's one of the reasons we need to put on the armor of God.

The belt of truth not only protects us but also guides us. It's our compass. "But when He, the Spirit of truth, comes, He will guide you into all the truth; for He will not speak on His own initiative, but whatever He hears, He will speak; and He will disclose to you what is to come" (John 16:13). If we surround ourselves with God's truth, Satan can't lead us down destructive paths. We get to enjoy all the good things that God has in store for us.

DIG DEEP

Some people argue that what's true for one person may not be true for someone else. But Jesus said, "I am the . . . truth" (John 14:6)—the *only* way to the life that God intends for us. Ask yourself the following questions and answer them truthfully:

1. What are some lies Satan uses to try to deceive you?
2. How does the Holy Spirit guide you in your daily life, and do you really listen to His truth?

DAY 6

Put On the Breastplate of Righteousness

Stand firm . . . having put on the breastplate of righteousness.
—EPHESIANS 6:14

IF YOU RECEIVE AN INVITATION TO A WHITE-TIE PARTY, you might need to borrow or rent an outfit. The same goes for Paul's instruction to "put on the breastplate of righteousness." No one has that kind of righteousness on their own. That's why in the armor of God the belt of truth goes on first. Without it we might be tempted to believe that our own righteousness is enough, because we wrongly think that God's righteousness counted toward us through faith is not enough.

Isaiah said, "All our righteous deeds are like a filthy garment" (Isaiah 64:6). Good works can do nothing to save us because God's righteousness is a gift from God Himself to those who believe. Paul said, "He made Him who knew no sin to be sin on our behalf, so that we might become the righteousness of God in Him" (2 Corinthians 5:21).

If we don't put on the breastplate of righteousness, we make ourselves vulnerable to Satan, who tries to make us doubt our own salvation. I have met many reborn Christians who doubt their salvation whenever they fall into sin, and some even get depressed. Reborn believers must choose to put on Christ's righteousness daily, and it should remind us to live righteous lives. Even though our deeds do not save us, they prove that our faith is real. When we become reborn Christians, we receive a new spiritual nature, which wants to love and serve Christ. This new nature makes us hate sin and we try not to give in to our fleshly desires.

That doesn't mean we're always perfect. But when we fall into temptation and sin, we feel bad about it, repent, and ask God to forgive us. And He does. John said, "If we confess our sins, He is faithful and righteous, so that He will forgive us our sins and cleanse us from all unrighteousness" (1 John 1:9).

Putting on the breastplate of righteousness helps us resist temptation because it means we put God first in our lives by sacrificing our fleshly desires. Jesus said, "Seek first His kingdom and His righteousness, and all these things will be provided to you" (Matthew 6:33), and to His disciples He said, "If anyone wants to come after Me, he must deny himself, take up his cross, and follow Me" (Matthew 16:24).

With the breastplate of righteousness, we also need to put on Jesus Christ. Paul said in Romans 13:14, "But put on the Lord Jesus Christ, and make no provision for the flesh in regard to its lusts." The more we become "conformed to the image of [God's] Son" (Romans 8:29), the more we make choices He would make.

—————————— DIG DEEP ——————————

God gave you the breastplate of righteousness the day He declared you as righteous through the blood of Jesus, and you need to wear it at all times. If you wear it, there is nothing Satan can do to make you doubt your salvation. Ask yourself the following questions and answer them truthfully:

1. Which attacks are you especially vulnerable to if you don't put on the breastplate of righteousness?
2. How is your life different when you're wearing the breastplate of righteousness?

Put On the Shoes of the Gospel of Peace

And having strapped on your feet the
preparation of the gospel of peace.
—EPHESIANS 6:1

THE "GOSPEL OF PEACE" MAY SOUND GENTLE AND HARM-less. The truth is, it's one of the pieces of spiritual armor that Satan fears most. The gospel of peace is what saved you—and what made you join the battle against him. It shines God's light on this dark world and sets people free from believing Satan's lies, threatening his control over this world.

The gospel of peace clearly lays out what we must believe to receive God's forgiveness and eternal life: "That Christ died for our sins according to the Scriptures, and that He was buried, and that He was raised on the third day according to the Scriptures" (1 Corinthians 15:3–4). The gospel of peace isn't watered down to make it more acceptable to you or those around you. It's nonnegotiable. We either accept it as is or we suffer the consequences.

The gospel of peace is the power of God that brings salvation to the world, one life at a time. That's why Paul connected it to the idea of readiness. Our work isn't finished when we receive the gospel of peace. We must also be prepared to share it with others. Paul told Timothy: "Preach the word; be ready in season and out of season; correct, rebuke, and exhort, with great patience and instruction" (2 Timothy 4:2).

If we do not share the gospel, then something is wrong with our walk with Christ. How can we keep silent when we know there are lost people slowly walking toward their death, toward hell? That is not love; it is selfishness to keep the good news to ourselves. Our readiness to share the gospel is a matter of eternal life and death. Paul asked, "How then are they to call on Him in whom they have not believed? How are they to believe in Him whom they have not heard? And how are they to hear without a preacher?" (Romans 10:14).

Satan tries to prevent us from sharing the gospel by using diversions and distractions. He wants to keep us too busy to put on the shoes of our armor. Too distracted to start a conversation about eternity. Too entertained in this world to realize when an opportunity comes for us to share the gospel. The devil wants us to be unprepared. Or intimidated. Or apathetic. He wants us to wait until tomorrow.

We can fight him by being ready: Ready with the words of Scripture. Ready with the right approach to get people's interest. Ready with the courage to speak up. Ready to listen to and follow the Holy Spirit's guidance.

The shoes of the gospel of peace not only protect us on the spiritual battlefield, but they also bring hope to people who desperately need it. That's why Paul said, "How beautiful are the feet of those who bring good news of good things!" (Romans 10:15).

DIG DEEP

Paul wasn't the only apostle who preached readiness. Peter said, "Sanctify Christ as Lord in your hearts, always being ready to make a defense to everyone who asks you to give an account for the hope that is in you" (1 Peter 3:15). Ask yourself the following questions and answer them truthfully:

1. What response would you give to someone who asked about the hope that is in you?
2. What sometimes keeps you from sharing the gospel of peace with others?
3. How can you be better prepared to share it?

Name It and Claim It?

"If you remain in Me, and My words remain in you, ask whatever you wish, and it will be done for you."
—JOHN 15:7

JESUS SAID THAT FAITH AS SMALL AS A MUSTARD SEED can move mountains (Matthew 17:20). But can it guarantee health, wealth, and success? Many pastors and church leaders would like you to believe it can. They teach what is known as the prosperity gospel—the idea that you can "name" what you want and then "claim" it by having enough faith.

The teachings of the prosperity gospel don't come from the Bible. The only way to make these teachings seem biblical is to take certain passages out of context and then ignore other large sections of Scripture that directly contradict the prosperity gospel. Doing so causes more than a few problems for reborn believers.

First, *the prosperity gospel convinces us that we are equal partners with God in deciding what we will or won't experience.* But that's a privilege not even Jesus claimed. On the night He was arrested, Jesus felt the full weight of what He was about to do on the cross. According to the teachings of the prosperity gospel, He could have named and claimed His way out of the crucifixion. Look at what He prayed instead: "My Father, if it is possible, let this cup pass from Me; yet not as I will, but as You will" (Matthew 26:39). Jesus expressed His request to God—and then submitted to the Father's will. How can anyone who claims to follow Him do anything else?

Second, *the prosperity gospel reduces God to a cosmic wish-granter* or a *"genie in a bottle."* Yet God is sovereign. He does exactly what He wants and answers to no one. No one can overrule Him. In the book of Daniel, King Nebuchadnezzar said, "All the inhabitants of the earth are of no account, but He does according to His will among the army of heaven and among the inhabitants of earth; and no one can fend off His hand or say to Him, 'What have You done?'" (Daniel 4:35). God does not put His will on hold to satisfy our desires. And we have no reason to ask Him to.

Third, *the prosperity gospel makes us lose sight of all that God can do in and through us.* He builds strength in us, makes us useful to others, and makes us more like Jesus through our struggles. God has something extraordinary planned for your life—you can't even imagine what it might be. Don't throw it away by focusing on material comfort and wealth. There is much to be gained through struggle. Paul wrote, "And not only this, but we also exult in our tribulations, knowing that tribulation brings about perseverance; and perseverance, proven character; and proven character, hope; and hope does not disappoint, because the love of God has been poured out within our hearts through the Holy Spirit who was given to us" (Romans 5:3–5).

DIG DEEP

The prosperity gospel claims that God wants you to be prosperous. God's Word says that He wants you to be obedient and to pray for things that are in His will for your life. Ask yourself the following questions and answer them truthfully:

1. How might the quest for prosperity get in the way of your obedience and purpose?
2. How have your struggles made you a more effective Christian?

Mismatched

Do not be mismatched with unbelievers; for what
do righteousness and lawlessness share together, or
what does light have in common with darkness?
—2 Corinthians 6:14

GOD CREATED US WITH A NEED FOR FRIENDSHIP AND then surrounded us with people to meet that need. Proverbs 18:24 says, "There is a friend who sticks closer than a brother."

While friendship has its place, it must not come at the expense of our relationship with Christ. Jesus said, "If anyone comes to Me and does not hate his own father, mother, wife, children, brothers, sisters, yes, and even his own life, he cannot be My disciple" (Luke 14:26). He wasn't telling us to abandon for no reason the people who love us. He was saying that we must be willing to sacrifice our relationship with anyone or anything that gets in the way of our relationship with Him.

Our need for friendship can cloud our judgment. In 2 Corinthians 6:14 being mismatched refers to relationships with unbelievers. One chapter later, Paul got to the heart of the matter: "Therefore, having these promises, beloved, let's cleanse ourselves from all defilement of flesh and spirit, perfecting holiness in the fear of God" (2 Corinthians 7:1).

That may seem extreme, but Jesus calls reborn Christians to an incredibly high standard. Peter said, "Like the Holy One who called you, be holy yourselves also in all your behavior; because it is written: 'You shall be holy, for I am holy'" (1 Peter 1:15–16). So where does that leave us in our friendships with people who have not accepted the call to holiness? There are two key takeaways from the Bible's teachings on friendships with unbelievers.

First, *set boundaries*. Galatians 5:16 says, "Walk by the Spirit, and you will not carry out the desire of the flesh." When it comes to unbelievers, we can be the friend they come to when they want someone to confide in. We can't be the friend they turn to when they want someone to lie for them or to get drunk with them.

We may not always be the friend they want us to be, but we can be the friend they need to bring them to the light. If both parties agree to respect those boundaries, we can build strong friendships despite being mismatched in our beliefs.

Second, *pay close attention to the direction of influence in our friendships*. Proverbs 13:20 says, "One who walks with wise people will be wise." God's wisdom can impact our friends' lives through us. People are usually more interested in what you have to say when they know you care about them. This is how you can share the gospel effectively.

But influence can run the opposite way as well. The more time we spend with someone, the more likely it is that some of that person's attitudes, habits, and likes and dislikes will rub off on us. We can have meaningful relationships with people who don't share our Christian beliefs. But we need to make sure that it's God's will, and we have to be vigilant about living in a Christlike way—for our sake and theirs.

DIG DEEP

God wants you to interact with unbelievers. Your responsibility is to keep those friendships in perspective. Ask yourself the following questions and answer them truthfully:

1. How can you set boundaries with your unbelieving friends?
2. What influence do you have in your friendships with unbelieving friends?

Comfort for the Anxious Spirit

Anxiety in a person's heart weighs it down,
but a good word makes it glad.
—**PROVERBS 12:25**

ANXIETY AFFECTS SOME 284 MILLION PEOPLE WORLD-
wide, and the numbers are growing at an alarming rate. The most devastating aspects of anxiety are how it isolates us, robs us of joy, makes us feel broken, and leaves us wondering where we can find healing.

The answer to healing is in God's Word. God has filled Scripture with promises that can soothe even the most anxious spirit. David, who was no stranger to anxiety, said, "LORD, You have searched me and known me. You know when I sit down and when I get up; You understand my thought from afar" (Psalm 139:1–2).

God sees what our anxiety does to us. But He doesn't just observe from a distance. He draws closer to us when we struggle. "The LORD is near to the brokenhearted and saves those who are crushed in spirit" (Psalm 34:18). God makes His presence known to us in unmistakable ways. He may use the comforting words of a friend. Or a moment of clarity in the midst of emotional chaos. Or a song that speaks exactly to our situation. Whatever the method, God's message is the same: *I am right here with you in this.*

The Lord draws close not just to comfort us but also to protect us, because emotional struggles are often signs of a spiritual attack. Anxiety does not come from the Spirit; it comes from the flesh. If we live in the Spirit, we will not have anxiety. Paul wrote, "God has not given us a spirit of timidity, but of power and love and discipline" (2 Timothy 1:7). Satan, on the other hand, uses a spirit of fear and uncertainty. He tries to convince us that life is too overwhelming, that we don't have the emotional strength to deal with our challenges. He amplifies our negative emotions so that they drown out everything else and leave us feeling hopeless.

No matter how dark things seem, there is always light. David said, "The LORD is my light and my salvation; whom should I fear? The LORD is the defense of my life; whom shall I dread?" (Psalm 27:1). God will not leave us in darkness. Instead, He cuts through our emotional fog to shine a light on one key truth: if we put God first in our lives, He will take care of our deepest needs.

Jesus said, "Do not worry then, saying, 'What are we to eat?' or 'What are we to drink?' or 'What are we to wear for clothing?' For the Gentiles eagerly seek all these things; for your heavenly Father knows that you need all these things. But seek first His kingdom and His righteousness, and all these things will be added to you" (Matthew 6:31–33). Two thousand years later, His words still have the power to soothe an anxious soul through the Spirit within us. Trust in God, not because of who you are but because of who He is.

———————— DIG DEEP ————————

David said to God, "When I am afraid, I will put my trust in You" (Psalm 56:3). Ask yourself the following questions and answer them truthfully:

1. In what ways are you not trusting God when you are anxious?
2. What does putting God first look like in your life?

The Living God

The fool has said in his heart, "There is no God."
—Psalm 53:1

ONE OF THE GREAT MYSTERIES FOR REBORN CHRISTIANS is how atheists can look at the amazing world around us and not see God's hand in it. Yet we must remember that one of the great mysteries for atheists is how reborn Christians can look at the pain and chaos of the world around us and continue to place our faith in an all-powerful God. The distance between these two perspectives gives us plenty of room for conversation with unbelievers about why we believe God exists.

We can start with three compelling reasons. First, *we see God's fingerprints all over creation.* Paul said, "Because that which is known about God is evident within them; for God made it evident to them. For since the creation of the world His invisible attributes, that is His eternal power and divine nature, have been clearly perceived, being understood by what has been made, so that they are without excuse" (Romans 1:19–20). The intricate design of the natural world points to a Creator who cares deeply about His work. No one can plead ignorance when it comes to God's existence because we're surrounded by proof of it.

Second, *we see the evidence of God in His Word.* Practically speaking, the Bible should not make sense. It was written by more than forty different people over a period of fifteen hundred years. Its writers had little in common: David was a shepherd. Luke was a doctor. They wrote in locations spread across two thousand miles. Some of them wrote biographies. Others wrote history, law, poetry, or prophecy. There is no earthly reason for the different parts of Scripture to fit together as one book. Yet they do, perfectly. And Paul explained why: "All Scripture is inspired by God and profitable for teaching, for rebuke, for correction, for training in righteousness" (2 Timothy 3:16).

Third, *we were born with a longing for Him.* Ecclesiastes 3:11 says that God "has also set eternity in their heart." Without Him we feel an emptiness we can't explain. We may try to fill it with personal accomplishments, material possessions, volunteer work, relationships with others, the pursuit of pleasure, or any number of other things. But the emptiness remains. That need for God buried deep within us is a powerful argument for His existence.

Fourth, *we see that pain can bring us closer to God.* We learn that something is wrong with this world and that we need a Savior. Pain and suffering caused by humans show us the evil within us, that we have no cure. If there is evil, then there must be good. We cannot blame God for the evil that man causes, because God is the only one who can set us free from pain and suffering.

———————————— DIG DEEP ————————————

David said to God, "When I consider Your heavens, the work of Your fingers, the moon and the stars, which You have ordained; what is man that You think of him, and the son of man that You are concerned about him?" (Psalm 8:3–4). He realized God's existence makes a profound difference in our lives. Ask yourself the following questions and answer them truthfully:

1. Why is it foolish to believe there is no God?
2. How does God make Himself known to you? What difference does that make in your life?
3. What is the difference between believing that God exists and believing in Him for salvation?

The Body of Christ

*For just as we have many parts in one body and all the body's
parts do not have the same function, so we, who are many,
are one body in Christ, and individually parts of one another.*
—ROMANS 12:4–5

THE INTRICATE DESIGN OF EACH PART OF THE HUMAN
body and the amazing way the parts work together point to a
Designer who is infinitely wiser and more powerful than we can
imagine. It's no wonder that Paul explained the unity of believers by
comparing it to the human body. Here are four takeaways from his
explanation.

First, *Christ is the head*. His words motivate us. His example
inspires us. His will guides us. "He is also the head of the body, the
church; and He is the beginning, the firstborn from the dead, so that
He Himself will come to have first place in everything" (Colossians
1:18). The body of Christ isn't led by a pastor or a group of church
leaders. Those people are merely other parts of the body—people like
us who have unique skills to contribute.

Second, *every body part is vital*. "For the body is not one part, but
many. If the foot says, 'Because I am not a hand, I am not a part of the
body,' it is not for this reason any less a part of the body. . . . God has
arranged the parts, each one of them in the body, just as He desired.
If they were all one part, where would the body be? But now there
are many parts, but one body" (1 Corinthians 12:14–15, 18–20). Some
parts of the body may have a higher profile than others, but that
doesn't make them more important than others.

Third, *the body suffers if one part doesn't do its part*. Paul said, "But speaking the truth in love, we are to grow up in all aspects into Him who is the head, that is Christ, from whom the whole body, being fitted and held together by what every joint supplies, according to the proper working of each individual part, causes the growth of the body for the building up of itself in love" (Ephesians 4:15–16). God equipped each of us to be a functioning part of the body of Christ. If we choose not to function, the body loses some of its strength and effectiveness.

Fourth, *the unified body of Christ is a powerful testimony to unbelievers*. There is no earthly reason why a group made up of so many different personalities should be able to thrive spiritually as one unit. So when unbelievers see a church growing, making a difference in the community, and sincerely following Christ's commands, they will take notice. Jesus said, "I am not asking on behalf of these alone, but also for those who believe in Me through their word, that they may all be one; just as You, Father, are in Me and I in You, that they also may be in Us, so that the world may believe that You sent Me" (John 17:20–21).

DIG DEEP

If you are a reborn Christian, you are an essential part of the body of Christ. Ask yourself the following questions and answer them truthfully:

1. Why is your role in the body of Christ important?
2. How can you work with other reborn Christians to show unity in Christ?

A Model Prayer

*It happened that while Jesus was praying in a certain place,
after He had finished, one of His disciples said to Him, "Lord,
teach us to pray just as John also taught his disciples."*
—LUKE 11:1

WHAT AN AMAZING OPPORTUNITY THE DISCIPLES HAD.
They took prayer lessons from the One who knew better than anyone else how to talk to our heavenly Father. The model prayer that
Jesus showed them in Matthew 6 has five parts, which can be worked
into any conversation we have with God.

The first is *worship*. "Hallowed be Your name" (verse 9) is the
phrase Jesus used. This sets the right tone for our prayer because it
shows we understand *who* it is we're talking to. Praise and worship
help us express what a privilege it is to enter God's presence.

The second part of prayer is *submission*. In heaven, everyone
and everything submits to God's will. That's why heaven is perfect.
When we pray for the same thing to happen on earth—"Your kingdom come. Your will be done" (verse 10)—we are telling God that
we will put aside our own desires and ambitions to pursue His will.

The third part of prayer is *provision*. "Give us this day our daily
bread" (verse 11) is a way of acknowledging that God provides for all
our needs. Sometimes He does it in extraordinary ways. Most of the
time He does it in ways that go unnoticed. Prayer gives us the chance
to notice and celebrate this provision. It also gives us the chance to
admit that we are completely dependent on God. He gives us bread
for our bodies and food for our souls to grow spiritually in Him. God

will help us grow spiritually because Scripture tells us that "He who began a good work" in us "will complete it by the day of Christ Jesus" (Philippians 1:6).

The fourth part of prayer is *forgiveness*. When we sin, we create obstacles in our relationship with God and we grieve the Holy Spirit. The only way to remove those obstacles is to confess, turn away from our sin, and ask for God's forgiveness. If we want to receive His forgiveness, we also have to forgive those who have wronged us, because we cannot expect God to forgive us if we do not forgive other people. "Forgive us our debts, as we also have forgiven our debtors" is the way Jesus put it in Matthew 6:12. Forgiveness allows us to live in peace not only with God but also with others.

The fifth part of prayer is *petition*. God is generous beyond measure. He will give us whatever we ask when we pray within His will—including protection from evil. The example Jesus gave us is, "Do not lead us into temptation, but deliver us from evil" (verse 13). God will give us the strength to resist when we are tempted. He will send His light when darkness surrounds us. He will equip us to carry out His will. All we have to do is ask.

DIG DEEP

One of the greatest privileges you have is being able to enter God's presence. Prayer puts you in direct contact with almighty God. Ask yourself the following questions and answer them truthfully:

1. Do you make enough time to pray to God?
2. Which part of Jesus' model prayer do you need to emphasize this week?

Capable and Equipped

*All Scripture is inspired by God and beneficial for
teaching, for rebuke, for correction, for training in
righteousness; so that the man or woman of God may
be fully capable, equipped for every good work.*
—2 TIMOTHY 3:16–17

WE LIVE IN AN AMAZING TIME. WE CAN ACCESS VAST
amounts of information with just a few keystrokes. Yet that creates
unrealistic expectations for most of us—especially when it comes to
life's most pressing questions. *Why did God let this happen? Why doesn't
He answer my prayer? What's His plan for my life?* We get frustrated and
discouraged when we don't receive immediate answers.

But look at 2 Timothy 3:16–17, which describes the process of
spiritual maturity: "teaching," "rebuke," "correction," and "training."
These things require time and effort. They call for patience and diligence. And they show us important truths about God and His Word.

First, *God wants us to rely on Him.* When Moses led the people
of Israel to the promised land, God provided just enough manna
every morning to sustain them for that day. God wants us as His
people to come to Him daily for our needs. He breathed out Scripture
because He wants us to turn to His Word every day for guidance and
wisdom.

Second, *the harder we search for something, the more valuable it
becomes to us.* Proverbs 2 compares the wisdom of God's Word to a
treasure. Like all good treasures, it's not easily discovered. We must
commit to searching the Scriptures daily. We have to dig, sift, and

dig some more. The harder we work to discover God's wisdom, the more we appreciate it when we find it.

Third, *spiritual maturity is rarely what we imagine.* Our quest for God's wisdom is often tied to a specific situation. We want to know how to deal with a pressing problem or receive guidance in making a decision. But God has something much bigger in mind. He wants to make us capable and equipped for every good work. So He gives us more than we ask for because He knows what we need. He shows us perspectives we could never see on our own. In 2 Corinthians 12:7–8, Paul said he prayed three times for God to take away the thorn in his flesh. Paul likely believed he could be a more effective Christian minister without his affliction. But God helped him see that his physical weakness actually made him a more effective minister.

Fourth, *God's timing is perfect.* He reveals His truths when we need them and when we are ready to understand and apply them. We may read a certain Bible passage the same way ten times in a row. But as time passes, we grow in our faith. When we are ready, God may reveal a piece of truth in the passage that we had never noticed before. That's how we grow. We plant the seeds by spending time in prayer and in God's Word. But ultimately God determines our rate of spiritual maturity when we abide in Him.

DIG DEEP

As we grow in spiritual maturity, we become more dependent on God. Ask yourself the following questions and answer them truthfully:

1. Do you change the Bible to fit in with your lifestyle, or do you change your life to fit in with the Bible?
2. How might God make you better equipped to serve Him?

Never Ever

"I will never desert you, nor will I ever abandon you."
—HEBREWS 13:5

THAT WORD "NEVER" CAN BE DIFFICULT FOR SOME OF US
to hear, especially if we've been abandoned by someone close to us.
But people aren't perfect. God is. His presence is constant. Hebrews
13:8 says, "Jesus Christ is the same yesterday and today, and forever."

If we can't feel God's presence, it may be because we're distracted
by busyness or overwhelmed by emotions. Our spiritual vision gets
blurry. Sometimes we turn our backs on Him to pursue our own
desires. But God never leaves us.

If we want to be constantly aware of God's presence, we need
to live right before God by pursuing holiness, studying the Bible,
and praying without ceasing. In the Old Testament we see Shadrach,
Meshach, and Abed-nego face a fiery furnace. We see David walk
onto a battlefield to face a fearsome giant. Then we see the same
David in Psalm 51:10–11 saying, "Create in me a clean heart, God,
and renew a steadfast spirit within me. Do not cast me away from
Your presence and do not take Your Holy Spirit from me." Those
heroes of Scripture knew they weren't alone. God was in the furnace.
God stood with David.

He stands with us, too, no matter what situations we face. He
gives us His promise in His Word. We believe it and act on it with
faith. Even though we can't see the future, we know that God will
work all things together for good to those who are called according
to His purpose. Even if we have to face death because of persecution,

we should not fear it, because it is God alone who decides when our time here on earth is done. Remember Paul's words: "For to me, to live is Christ, and to die is gain" (Philippians 1:21).

Prayer reveals God's closeness in an even more immediate way. He doesn't rush to our side when we pray because He doesn't need to—He's already within us. Instead, He makes His presence known to us. He speaks to us. He listens to us and calms our spirit. He lets us know that we are never alone.

A great example of this is found in the story of Elisha in 2 Kings 6. Israel was at war with Aram. Elisha's servant awoke to find that the entire city was surrounded by Aramean soldiers. There was no way out. His first instinct was to panic. Elisha prayed, "Lord, please, open his eyes so that he may see" (verse 17). God allowed the servant to see the heavenly army that protected Elisha—an entire mountain filled with horses and chariots of fire.

Elisha's prayer allowed his servant to see what Elisha already knew: God and His forces were not only much bigger and more powerful than his enemies but they were also much closer than anyone would have imagined. Having that confidence allowed Elisha to serve God in a powerful way. It can do the same for us.

DIG DEEP

Joshua 1:9 says, "Be strong and courageous! Do not be terrified nor dismayed, for the Lord your God is with you wherever you go." Ask yourself the following questions and answer them truthfully:

1. What causes you to lose sight of God's presence in your life?
2. Is there something God wants you to do that you are too afraid to pursue?

Christians Aren't Boring

"I came so that they may have life, and have it abundantly."
—JOHN 10:10

ONE OF THE MOST COMMON STEREOTYPES ABOUT Christians is that we lead dull lives. In many people's minds, saying yes to God means saying no to excitement. Fear of boredom can keep unbelievers from seeking to learn more about the gospel. Christians can help others see that the life God calls us to is not just fulfilling but also exciting.

The truth is, reborn believers are interesting because *our joy and peace are unconditional.* They don't depend on our circumstances. Even when everything seems to be going wrong, we can be filled with joy and peace. Even after losing my father and two brothers, I have joy and peace that I cannot explain. Paul wrote about this kind of joy and peace that can only be found in Christ: "Rejoice in the Lord always; again I will say, rejoice! Let your gentle spirit be known to all people. The Lord is near. Be anxious for nothing, but in everything by prayer and pleading with thanksgiving let your requests be made known to God. And the peace of God, which surpasses all comprehension, will guard your hearts and minds in Christ Jesus" (Philippians 4:4–7).

Christians are also interesting because *we ask tough questions about life*, such as, *Where did we come from? Why is there evil in the world? What is my purpose? Does anyone truly love me? Where is God when I feel lonely or afraid? How can I know for sure that I'm going to heaven?* God's Word is filled with answers, and He encourages us to seek Him when we have questions: "Call to Me and I will answer you, and I will tell you great and mighty things, which you do not know" (Jeremiah 33:3).

Believers are also interesting because *we have fellowship*. The connection among God's people is unlike any other relationship. Look at this description of the early church: "They were continually devoting themselves to the apostles' teaching and to fellowship, to the breaking of bread and to prayer. Everyone kept feeling a sense of awe; and many wonders and signs were taking place through the apostles. . . . And the Lord was adding to their number day by day those who were being saved" (Acts 2:42, 43, 47). Circumstances have changed in the past two thousand years, but not the Spirit of God, who is within all believers and is present when we gather in fellowship.

Reborn believers inspire one another to be bold in living our faith. We confront one another in a spirit of love. We lift up those who fall. We hold one another accountable. We grow together. We celebrate and mourn together. We work together in an amazing way, like different parts of a single body. And there's nothing boring about that.

DIG DEEP

You can help people see beyond stereotypes through how you live your faith. Ask yourself the following questions and answer them truthfully:

1. Can unbelievers see God's unconditional peace in your life, or are you trying to find peace from things in this temporary world?
2. Why might an unbeliever be interested in the fellowship you enjoy?

The Problem with Hypocrisy

*They profess to know God, but by their deeds
they deny Him, being detestable and disobedient
and worthless for any good deed.*
—TITUS 1:16

WHEN A VISITING SPORTS TEAM ENTERS A STADIUM OR arena, they expect some of the spectators to root against them. As Christians, we're the visiting team in this world. Peter said we are "foreigners and strangers" (1 Peter 2:11). Nothing makes people root harder against Christians than hypocrisy. Many people see Christianity as a show, a scam designed to control people's minds and wallets. They see us as concerned only with outside appearances, as people who say one thing and do another. News stories of church leaders caught in sex scandals and one's personal experiences with churchgoers who are less than loving feed unbelievers' hatred of hypocrisy.

If we want to change their minds, we need to understand a few things about hypocrisy. The first is that *many people who are guilty of hypocrisy say they are Christians but aren't truly reborn believers.* Paul said, "For such men are false apostles, deceitful workers, disguising themselves as apostles of Christ. No wonder, for even Satan disguises himself as an angel of light. Therefore it is not surprising if his servants also disguise themselves as servants of righteousness, whose end will be according to their deeds" (2 Corinthians 11:13–15). These people hurt the reputations of the Christians around them.

The second thing we need to understand is that *we're all guilty of hypocrisy.* Jesus holds His followers to a high standard, and sometimes we fall short of that standard. Paul said, "All have sinned and fall short of the glory of God" (Romans 3:23). Sometimes we fall short in a very public way, doing damage not just to our own testimony but to people's perceptions of Christianity. We give unbelievers reason to be cynical about our witness. We make it harder to minister to them. And that brings us to the third thing to remember.

To undo the damage, we must be transparent about our struggles to live as Paul instructed in Ephesians 4:1–3: "Walk in a manner worthy of the calling with which you have been called, with all humility and gentleness, with patience, bearing with one another in love, being diligent to keep the unity of the Spirit in the bond of peace." We can't pretend to have it all together when we really don't. We can't look at the speck in someone else's eye when we have a log in our own (Matthew 7:3). The true church of God is full of people who understand that even their best deeds are like filthy rags to a holy God. We can never save ourselves, which is why Jesus died for us on the cross. Now, out of love for Him, we do our best to obey His will through the Holy Spirit, who gives us the strength to overcome sin. If we are open and humble about the challenges we face, we lessen our risk of being seen as hypocrites.

——————————— DIG DEEP ———————————

When you talk with unbelievers who want nothing to do with Christians, acknowledge your own sinfulness and struggles, but remind them about the difference between who you are now and who you used to be without God in your life. Ask yourself the following questions and answer them truthfully:

1. How would you describe the standard that Jesus holds you to?
2. How would you describe your own struggles with hypocrisy?

Judge Not?

"Do not judge by the outward appearance,
but judge with righteous judgment."
—JOHN 7:24

IF YOU EVER WANT TO PROVOKE A STRONG REACTION IN unbelievers, ask this question: Do you think Christians are judgmental? The response will probably be overwhelming, and you might not know how to react. Here are four things to consider.

First, *people who say Christians are judgmental are right.* Paul said, "The fruit of the Spirit is love, joy, peace, patience, kindness, goodness, faithfulness, gentleness, self-control; against such things there is no law" (Galatians 5:22–23). But that fruit isn't always apparent in believers' lives. Many use their faith like a weapon. Others use it to make themselves look better. They misrepresent God's message and make it difficult for other believers to minister, poisoning the waters of evangelism with their judgmental attitude.

Second, *the Christian message is unpopular.* Many people would like to believe that Jesus taught love and acceptance and nothing else. But the reality is, He called people to repent and obey. "No, I tell you, but unless you repent, you will all likewise perish" (Luke 13:3).

No matter how careful we are not to sound judgmental, people don't want to be told that they're sinners in need of salvation. Or that their good works are nothing more than filthy rags (Isaiah 64:6), as far as God is concerned. Jesus said, "And this is the judgment, that the Light has come into the world, and people loved the darkness rather than the Light; for their deeds were evil" (John 3:19).

We must get used to the idea that people will reject what we have to say. If some people rejected Jesus when He shared the truth, the same will happen when we do it. Jesus warned His followers, "Woe to you when all the people speak well of you; for their fathers used to treat the false prophets the same way" (Luke 6:26).

Third, *our job is to speak the truth in love.* That's how Paul put it in Ephesians 4:15. The truth isn't always easy to hear, but that shouldn't keep us from trying to speak it in the most effective way possible. People can sense when we have their best interests at heart.

Speaking the truth in love is the antidote to speaking the truth in judgment. When we approach people with a judgmental attitude through the flesh, we put ourselves above them. When we approach them through the Spirit and in love, we put ourselves on their level. We're giving them the same message that was given to us.

Fourth, *a humble attitude goes a long way.* Paul said, "Do nothing from selfishness or empty conceit, but with humility consider one another as more important than yourselves; do not merely look out for your own personal interests, but also for the interests of others" (Philippians 2:3–4). That's a ministry goal to strive for. Your soul— with your emotions, will, and intellect—needs to be guided by the Spirit at all times. God's Spirit combined with a humble attitude is a powerful combination.

DIG DEEP

Before judging others, act through the Spirit with love. Ask yourself the following questions and answer them truthfully:

1. What kind of damage has been caused in your own life, or in the lives of those close to you, by judgmental Christians?
2. How can you speak a difficult truth in a loving way?

Lovable

Give thanks to the God of heaven, for His
lovingkindness is everlasting.
—PSALM 136:26

DOES GOD LOVE ME FOR WHO I AM? IF YOU'VE EVER asked that question, you were probably experiencing pain or self-doubt. Or maybe you've always felt like you had to earn love from other people, and you assumed the same was true with God.

The Bible has great news for anyone who's ever wondered whether they are lovable in God's eyes. God said, "Before I formed you in the womb I knew you" (Jeremiah 1:5). He formed you as you are and was pleased by His work. He lovingly stitched together every part of you before you were born. You bear the mark of His workmanship.

You may worry that certain secret things you do or think would make you unlovable to God if He knew about them. But He does know about them. David said, "You know when I sit down and when I get up; You understand my thought from far away" (Psalm 139:2). Nothing is hidden from God's sight. His feelings for you aren't based on the way you act in church or when you're with your Christian friends. He sees everything—the good and the bad. And He still loves you. This does not mean that He approves of your sin; He hates sin. But He loves you, which is why Jesus died in your place on the cross.

If you've ever been abandoned by someone you love, you may worry that God's love is temporary too. Or that it depends on His mood or feelings on a given day. But God's love is constant. He will never walk away or leave you alone. Paul said, "I am convinced that neither death, nor life, nor angels, nor principalities, nor things present, nor things to come, nor powers, nor height, nor depth, nor any other created thing will be able to separate us from the love of God that is in Christ Jesus our Lord" (Romans 8:38–39). You can invest every bit of yourself in God without fear. He's not going anywhere.

If you've ever been in a toxic relationship, you may believe that God's love requires sacrifice and suffering on your part. But He is the One who sacrificed and suffered when He gave His only Son to die in our place so that we could live forever with Him. Every one of us has rejected God and chosen to go our own way. "But God demonstrates His own love toward us, in that while we were still sinners, Christ died for us" (Romans 5:8).

If you've ever been in an aimless relationship, you may believe that God's love doesn't necessarily lead anywhere. But that's not the case. God's love isn't passive; it's incredibly active. He has mapped out an amazing course for your life: "But just as it is written: 'Things which eye has not seen and ear has not heard, and which have not entered the human heart, all that God has prepared for those who love Him'" (1 Corinthians 2:9).

That's how much God loves you.

DIG DEEP

God loves you. Those three simple words have the power to change lives forever. Ask yourself the following questions and answer them truthfully:

1. What might cause you to wonder whether you're lovable?
2. Do you truly love God unconditionally, the way He loves you? How do you know?
3. Who in your life needs to hear that God loves them?

Jesus Is God

"I and the Father are one."
—JOHN 10:30

SOME PEOPLE DOUBT THE CHRISTIAN FAITH AND ARGUE that Jesus never claimed to be God. Their arguments strike at the heart of our beliefs, because if Jesus isn't God, He doesn't have the power to save us from our sins. His death on the cross accomplished nothing. His teachings have no special importance. If Jesus isn't God, eternal life is beyond our reach. And this world is all we have to look forward to.

But we don't have to worry about any of those dark scenarios because Jesus *is* God. He made that clear during His earthly ministry. Jesus' enemies certainly understood that He claimed to be God, as He told them, "I and the Father are one" (John 10:30). He also said, "Truly, truly I say to you, before Abraham was born, I am" (John 8:58). Those last two words, "I am," were the same ones that Jesus used to reveal Himself to Moses (Exodus 3:14). Using them was considered the worst kind of blasphemy.

In these incidents and others, the reactions of Jesus' enemies were the same: "For this reason therefore the Jews were seeking all the more to kill Him, because He not only was breaking the Sabbath, but also was calling God His own Father, making Himself equal with God" (John 5:18).

On the night of Jesus' arrest, the Jewish high priest asked Him directly, "Are You the Christ, the Son of the Blessed One?" (Mark 14:61). In other words, "Are You God?" Crucifixion hung in the balance. If Jesus had said no, He would have escaped the worst physical, emotional, and spiritual agony that anyone ever faced.

Instead, He answered, "I am; and you shall see the Son of Man sitting at the right hand of power, and coming with the clouds of heaven" (Mark 14:62). Not only did He acknowledge His identity as sovereign God but He also warned that one day He would return to judge those who were judging Him. That was the final straw, as far as His enemies were concerned. Jesus was taken away to be beaten and crucified.

Jesus is not just a man who existed in the New Testament. He is God and creation itself came into being through Him (John 1:1–3). There is another, less dramatic example in Scripture that helps us understand why it's important to know that Jesus is God. In John 14, Jesus' disciple Philip made a bold request. On behalf of the other disciples, he asked Jesus to show them God the Father. Jesus said, "The one who has seen Me has seen the Father" (verse 9).

When the time came for God to set His plan of salvation in motion, He didn't recruit a prophet to go around telling people what He was like and what He wanted from us. Instead, He stepped out of heaven and came to earth in human form to live among us. He said, "You want to know what I'm like? Watch what I do. Listen to what I say. Follow the example I set."

Jesus left no doubt in the minds of His followers that He is God.

DIG DEEP

Jesus asked His disciples, "Who do you yourselves say that I am?" (Matthew 16:15). It's a question every one of us must answer. Ask yourself the following questions and answer them truthfully:

1. How do you know that Jesus is God?
2. What can we learn about God from Jesus' life on earth?

Don't Give Up

But you, be strong and do not lose courage,
for there is reward for your work.
—2 Chronicles 15:7

THE DIFFERENCE BETWEEN SUCCESS AND FAILURE IS often a matter of perspective and perseverance. Some people want us to believe that every setback is a failure, something to be ashamed of. The truth is, every setback is a learning experience, something that can make us wiser—if we let it. Thomas Edison said, "I have not failed. I've just found ten thousand ways that won't work."

That's the perspective of someone who knows what it takes to ultimately succeed. Every way that didn't work taught Edison more about the problems he faced and the resources he needed to overcome them. That perspective inspired him to persevere. To try again for the five thousandth and the ten thousandth time. The book of Proverbs gives us a similar perspective: "For a righteous person falls seven times, and rises again, but the wicked stumble in time of despair" (Proverbs 24:16).

For reborn believers, perspective and perseverance in the midst of failure are especially important. After all, unbelievers are watching us. They want to see the difference Jesus makes in our lives when we're at our lowest. They want to see how we deal with failure.

That's where perseverance comes in. On the night Jesus was arrested, Peter failed miserably in a very public way (Matthew 26:69–75). Hours after promising Jesus that he would stay faithful no matter what, Peter panicked when someone recognized him as one of Jesus' followers. Instead of telling the truth and facing the consequences, Peter lied. He denied even knowing Jesus—and not just once or twice. Three times that night Peter had an opportunity to take a bold stand for Jesus, and three times he failed.

After his third denial Peter felt intense guilt and shame, and he repented for what he had done. Then he did something else: he showed up. He didn't hide. He didn't let his embarrassment get the best of him. He didn't worry about what people were saying behind his back. When the disciples gathered again, Peter showed up. When he heard that Jesus' tomb was empty, he showed up there, too, as fast as he could.

Peter persevered. He refused to let his failure define him. He restored his relationship with Jesus. He reset his focus on serving Him. When Jesus returned to heaven, Peter stepped into a key leadership role in building the church and spreading Jesus' message. He helped change the world, something that probably would have seemed unimaginable to him on the night of Jesus' arrest.

A simple fisherman turned apostle discovered the truth that every believer who has ever failed needs to understand: success is much sweeter to those who have persevered through failure. That's why Paul said, "Let's not become discouraged in doing good, for in due time we will reap, if we do not become weary" (Galatians 6:9).

DIG DEEP

Failure makes you more relatable to other people. Everyone wants to know they're not alone when they fail. Ask yourself the following questions and answer them truthfully:

1. How can you make your personal experiences with failure part of your Christian testimony?
2. What does showing up after you fail look like in your life?

Hold On

*Our soul waits for the LORD; He is our help and
our shield. For our heart rejoices in Him, because
we trust in His holy name. Let Your favor, O LORD,
be upon us, just as we have waited for You.*
—PSALM 33:20–22

STRANGE AND TERRIBLE THINGS HAPPEN WHEN EMO-
tional darkness fills our horizon. Reality becomes distorted. The
distance between us and the people who care about us seems to
expand. Problems that once seemed manageable grow and multiply
until they threaten to overwhelm us. The bright things in life that
used to bring us joy and happiness start to dim.

And then the voices start. The ones in our head that tell us there's
no way out. Or that life's not worth the trouble. Or that the world
would be better off without us.

They're all lies from our fleshly nature and the devil, and God's
Word pushes back hard against them. Jesus said, "The thief comes
only to steal and kill and destroy; I came so that they would have
life, and have it abundantly" (John 10:10). The urge to destroy and
end things comes from our enemy. Satan comes like a thief to steal
our joy and destroy our lives. He twists the truth to achieve his goals
and twists our emotions and our perspective. Our enemy makes us
see bad things that aren't there and overlook good things that are.

Jesus, on the other hand, shows us how rewarding life can be. He
is not content merely to give us life—average, unremarkable, plain
life. No, Jesus came so that we can have life abundantly. He pours out

His blessings for us to enjoy. He opens doors to amazing opportunities. He fills our life to the brim.

The life Jesus offers is not free of pain and struggles. There are high highs and low lows. We can expect to laugh, cry, and mourn. Through it all, though, we can have peace, hope, and a sense of purpose. God will use it for good if we put Him first in our lives and trust Him with everything.

Look at what He told those who were taken into exile from Jerusalem to Bablyon: "'For I know the plans that I have for you,' declares the LORD, 'plans for prosperity and not for disaster, to give you a future and a hope'" (Jeremiah 29:11). No matter how dark the horizon seems at a given moment, it's only temporary.

Of course, it's not always easy to look past the dark horizon. Sometimes our circumstances are too much for us to bear alone. Jesus understands that too. That's why He said, "Come to Me, all who are weary and burdened, and I will give you rest" (Matthew 11:28). The Lord wants us to turn to Him when life gets rough. He will not turn His back or give us more than we can handle through Him. He knows exactly what burdens we're carrying, and He's strong enough to shoulder every one of them.

DIG DEEP

The abundant life that Jesus offers is not trouble-free. But it promises ultimate meaning, purpose, and fulfillment. Ask yourself the following questions and answer them truthfully:

1. What is the difference between normal life and abundant life in Christ?
2. What burdens are you carrying right now that you need to give to Jesus?

A Source of Comfort

Blessed be the God and Father of our Lord Jesus Christ,
the Father of mercies and God of all comfort, who
comforts us in all our affliction so that we will be able to
comfort those who are in any affliction with the comfort
with which we ourselves are comforted by God.
—2 CORINTHIANS 1:3–4

COMFORT IS SUCH A PRECIOUS RESOURCE. WE ALL NEED somewhere to turn, something to make us feel better and give us perspective when we face difficulties in life. We need God's Word. We need to trust in it and act on it. In a single sentence in the passage above, Paul gave us three crucial truths to remember about comfort.

The first is that *God will not always keep us from affliction.* Paul understood this better than anyone. He suffered from many difficulties and an ongoing affliction that he wanted God to remove. God chose not to. Instead, God helped Paul see that He could show His strength through this weakness. "Concerning this I implored the Lord three times that it might leave me. And He has said to me, 'My grace is sufficient for you, for power is perfected in weakness.' Most gladly, therefore, I will rather boast about my weaknesses, so that the power of Christ may dwell in me" (2 Corinthians 12:8–9).

God wants us to pray about everything, including being delivered from affliction. Experiencing trials and pain is a common life experience, and He can answer our prayer with a "yes," "wait," or "no."

God can do amazing things in and through us, even in the worst of circumstances. Psalm 23, one of the most famous passages in the Bible, highlights this truth. David said, "Even though I walk through the valley of the shadow of death, I fear no evil, for You are with me; Your rod and Your staff, they comfort me" (verse 4). Notice that God didn't steer him away from the valley of the shadow of death—and all the suffering that goes with it. He walked David straight into and through affliction.

And that brings us to the second truth. *God is present every step of the way to comfort and guide us.* He walks with us through the affliction. The closer we draw to Him, through prayer and the comforting words of Scripture, the more we sense His presence. James said, "Come close to God and He will come close to you" (James 4:8).

The third truth is that *He comforts us in affliction so that we can comfort others.* This is how God makes disciples of us. John said, "We love, because He first loved us" (1 John 4:19). Likewise, we comfort because He first comforted us. He showed us the path through the valley of the shadow of death so that we can show others.

--------------------- **DIG DEEP** ---------------------

If you learn from your own afflictions how to comfort others, you will become an extremely valuable resource to the people around you. Ask yourself the following questions and answer them truthfully:

1. When have you sensed God's presence in the midst of your own affliction?
2. How willing are you to endure hardship when God puts you through trials and tribulations to teach you something?
3. How has God equipped you to help others who need comfort?

Growing Through Bible Study

*For the word of God is living and active, and sharper
than any two-edged sword, even penetrating as far as the
division of soul and spirit, of both joints and marrow, and
able to judge the thoughts and intentions of the heart.*
—HEBREWS 4:12

PERHAPS YOU'VE SEEN YOUTUBE CLIPS OF OLD MEN WHO
show up at basketball courts and amaze the other players with their
skills and speed. The prank is that they aren't really old men at all but
rather world-class players in disguise.

These video clips serve as a perfect introduction to a discussion
of God's Word. If you were to ask people who don't know much about
the Bible to describe it, many would probably say, "It's an ancient
book that really isn't relevant to life in the twenty-first century."

The writer of Hebrews told a different story. Although the Bible
was written thousands of years ago, it's more alive and active than
we can possibly imagine. Like the old men in the video clips, it can
amaze us in unexpected ways. There are three things we need to
remember about God's Word that will help us see it with the right
perspective.

First, *it's everything we need*. Peter said that God's "divine power
has granted to us everything pertaining to life and godliness" (2 Peter
1:3). Everything we need to know about justification, sanctification,
discovering God's will, finding true fulfillment, coming back from
failure, building lasting relationships, and countless other relevant
topics can be found in the pages of Scripture.

Second, *it comes from God Himself.* In a culture where almost anything can be faked, it's hard to know where to put our trust. Paul said, "All Scripture is inspired by God and profitable for teaching, for rebuke, for correction, for training in righteousness; so that the man or woman of God may be fully capable for every good work" (2 Timothy 3:16–17). The entire Bible came from God Himself, who cannot lie. That makes it the standard of truth.

God's Word is the measuring rod we use to determine false teachings and empty philosophies. John said, "Beloved, do not believe every spirit, but test the spirits to see whether they are from God, because many false prophets have gone out into the world" (1 John 4:1). The test is simple: anyone or anything that contradicts the Bible should not be trusted.

Third, *it makes us better.* The writer of Hebrews described God's Word as a blade that cuts us open all the way to the heart. At first glance, it's hard to imagine what good could come from an instrument so dangerous and intrusive—unless that instrument is a scalpel in the hands of a skilled surgeon.

That's what God's Word is. It cuts right between the bone and marrow, clearly showing us the difference between the old sinful flesh and the new spiritual nature that we have received from God. The more we read Scripture, the more we allow its blade to reach to the deepest parts of our heart, soul, and spirit and cut away the things that pose a danger to our spiritual health.

DIG DEEP

You need the truth of Scripture to grow and change into the likeness of Christ. Ask yourself the following questions and answer them truthfully:

1. How much time do you spend reading God's Word every week?
2. How many times have you read the entire Bible?

Growing Through Prayer

Pray without ceasing.
—1 Thessalonians 5:17

IF YOU'VE EVER DONE ANYTHING "WITHOUT CEASING" for any length of time, you know it can get old pretty quickly. The challenge for us is to pray without ceasing while not allowing our prayers to get stale. The good news is, God's Word offers valuable tips on how to keep our prayers fresh, interesting, and powerful.

Be awestruck. As amazing as it seems, God takes pleasure in our worship. He wants to hear how much He means to us. Before we pray, it's helpful to remind ourselves that we're in the presence of the Creator. We're having a one-on-one conversation with God Himself. Isaiah was good at this. "Do you not know? Have you not heard? The Everlasting God, the Lord, the Creator of the ends of the earth does not become weary or tired. His understanding is inscrutable" (Isaiah 40:28). Once we understand what a privilege prayer is, we can pray more effectively.

Be repentant. Our sin puts up a barrier between us and God. Repenting and asking for His forgiveness clears it away. David was good at this. "Be gracious to me, God, according to Your faithfulness; according to the greatness of Your compassion, wipe out my wrong-doings. Wash me thoroughly from my guilt and cleanse me from my sin" (Psalm 51:1–2). Once the barrier is removed, we can go deeper into conversation with God.

Be thankful. There's no way to thank God for everything He does, but that shouldn't stop us from trying. Paul said, "In everything give thanks; for this is God's will for you in Christ Jesus" (1 Thessalonians 5:18). A thankful heart is an observant heart, and an observant heart is a joyful heart. To be truly grateful for the things God has given us, we have to notice them. As we do that over and over, we start to cultivate a spirit of joy.

Be yourself. God doesn't grade our grammar or the length of our prayers. He looks at our hearts. Jesus warned, "And when you are praying, do not use thoughtless repetition as the Gentiles do, for they think that they will be heard because of their many words" (Matthew 6:7).

Be aware of your motives. God invites us to take our requests to Him. But that doesn't mean He gives us everything we ask for. James said there's a reason for that: "You ask and do not receive, because you ask with wrong motives, so that you may spend what you request on your pleasures" (James 4:3). God knows what we want and why. And when our desires and motives line up with His, amazing things happen.

Be quiet. There are times when God gives you the answer to your prayer or peace through the Holy Spirit when He hears your prayer, which means you can stop praying or you're wasting your time. You only need to pray until you have a breakthrough. There are times to pray and times to listen. Let God speak to you. Jesus said, "The one who is of God hears the words of God" (John 8:47).

DIG DEEP

To pray effectively, you have to understand who God is and how best to approach Him. Ask yourself the following questions and answer them truthfully:

1. How do you approach God?
2. What keeps your prayer life from being more effective?
3. How can you hear God's voice when you pray?

Growing Through Fellowship

What we have seen and heard we proclaim to you also, so that you too may have fellowship with us; and indeed our fellowship is with the Father, and with His Son Jesus Christ.
—1 John 1:3

IN ANY CAST OF CHARACTERS YOU'LL FIND A LONE WOLF— the self-reliant antihero who lives by his own rules, doesn't play well with others, and goes his own way. And audiences go wild for him. There's something about the brooding loner that appeals to people's imaginations.

For reborn believers, however, the appeal of the lone wolf stops at the church door. God's plan is for His people to work as a community. We thrive and grow through fellowship, and the key ingredient in fellowship is love. Jesus said to His followers, "I am giving you a new commandment, that you love one another; just as I have loved you, that you also love one another" (John 13:34).

We can offer numerous legitimate-sounding reasons not to love other people. They lie. They cheat. They cause trouble. But guess what? So do we, and we still fail at times even as Christians. Romans 5:8 says, "God demonstrates His own love toward us, in that while we were still sinners, Christ died for us." Suddenly our reasons don't sound legitimate anymore, do they?

The love that makes fellowship possible isn't based on feelings. Jesus didn't say, "Find something to love in one another." He said, "Love one another." Agape love is an act of your will, not based on a feeling. You have to choose to love others, including your enemies, even when your flesh does not want to. You do this through the Spirit. Love starts with our actions and attitudes by giving one another our time and energy.

Let's look at the benefits of fellowship. First, *good things happen when we spend time with other believers.* Hebrews 10:24–25 says, "Let's consider how to encourage one another in love and good deeds, not abandoning our own meeting together, as is the habit of some people, but encouraging one another." The bond that is created through fellowship can encourage us to act more boldly and take our walk with Christ more seriously. Fellowship allows us to see other people using their spiritual gifts and prompts us to use ours.

Second, *fellowship also protects us from our enemy,* who Peter described as a "roaring lion, seeking someone to devour" (1 Peter 5:8)—a predator. When predators hunt, they look for vulnerable, individual prey—ones who have been separated from their herd. The lone wolf (or sheep or wildebeest or reborn believer) is a prime target. There is safety in the herd, and there is safety in fellowship.

Finally, *fellowship unites us in a way few other things can.* Paul said, "For by one Spirit we were all baptized into one body, whether Jews or Greeks, whether slaves or free, and we were all made to drink of one Spirit" (1 Corinthians 12:13). The artificial barriers that divide us in other walks of life have no place in the body of Christ. Fellowship is too important for us to allow anything to get in the way.

DIG DEEP

Fellowship requires effort, patience, and understanding. God will reward your effort. Ask yourself the following questions and answer them truthfully:

1. What are the challenges you face when it comes to fellowship?
2. How seriously do you follow Paul's instruction for believers to "consider one another as more important than yourselves" (Philippians 2:3)?

Growing Through Testifying

*"Go, therefore, and make disciples of all the
nations, baptizing them in the name of the
Father and the Son and the Holy Spirit."*
—MATTHEW 28:19

THINK OF THE LAST TIME YOU GOT REALLY GOOD NEWS.
If you're like most people, you wanted to share it. That's what testifying is: sharing good news. And that's what Jesus called His followers to do in Matthew 28. He wants us to talk about the good news—the gospel—that changed our lives, so that through it others might be saved as well. This is not an option; we've been commanded to share the gospel to the ends of the earth.

Unfortunately, the thought of testifying is scary to a lot of reborn Christians, because they care more about what people might think about them than what God wants them to do. For some of us, sharing something so intensely personal makes us vulnerable to rejection and ridicule. We must learn to face our fleshly fears.

Paul often faced physical danger because of his commitment to share the good news of Christ. Yet nothing stopped him from sharing: "For I am not ashamed of the gospel, for it is the power of God for salvation to everyone who believes, to the Jew first and also to the Greek" (Romans 1:16). We need to remind ourselves that souls are at stake. If we truly love people, we will care about where they will end up for all eternity.

One of the best ways to work through our fear is to let the Holy Spirit lead us. Jesus promised His followers, "But the Helper, the Holy

Spirit, whom the Father will send in My name, He will teach you all things, and remind you of all that I said to you" (John 14:26). When we sense an opportunity to share our faith, we can ask God to calm our fleshly fears and help us follow the Holy Spirit's lead.

He will help us know how and when to share the good news in truth and in love. God will also remind us to listen, a highly under-rated skill when it comes to testifying. "Everyone must be quick to hear, slow to speak, and slow to anger" (James 1:19). The more we know about someone's background, struggles, hopes, and fears, the greater impact we can have in sharing the gospel with them. The best way to learn those things is by listening.

And when it's time for us to share the message of Christ, we must remember the importance of keeping it simple. That's the approach Peter took when he spoke to the Jewish leaders of Jerusalem about Jesus: "And there is salvation in no one else; for there is no other name under heaven that has been given among men by which we must be saved" (Acts 4:12).

DIG DEEP

God has given every reborn Christian the opportunity and responsibility to share the gospel throughout the world so that whoever believes in Jesus will have eternal life. Ask yourself the following questions and answer them truthfully:

1. When was the last time you shared the gospel with someone?
2. How can you become more confident in sharing the gospel?

Ever Ready

Sanctify Christ as Lord in your hearts, always being ready to make a defense to everyone who asks you to give an account for the hope that is in you.
—1 PETER 3:15

WE CAN PREPARE FOR BAD WEATHER BY STAYING INSIDE our homes and ensuring our windows and doors are secured. We can prepare for retirement by investing wisely. But how can we prepare to defend our faith when someone asks us to explain where our hope comes from?

First, *we can learn how to best use God's Word.* Paul instructed Timothy, "Be diligent to present yourself approved to God as a workman who does not need to be ashamed, accurately handling the word of truth" (2 Timothy 2:15). A craftsman knows exactly what tools to use for a specific job. We learn to accurately handle God's Word by studying it. We find out how passages connect to one another and how they apply to the situations we face in our lives. We learn by asking tough questions and digging for the answers. We learn by memorizing passages that hold special meaning for us.

Second, *we can anticipate questions that people might ask.* Let's face it, there are Christian teachings that make no sense to unbelievers. The first will be last? Love your enemies? Turn the other cheek? Why would anyone choose to live like that?

And then there are the more basic questions: How do you know God exists? Why should we trust the Bible? Why is Jesus the only way to God? If we've wrestled with those questions ourselves, we can share the explanations that made sense to us. If not, we can pray about them. In Jeremiah 33:3, God said, "Call to Me and I will answer you, and I will tell you great and mighty things, which you do not know."

Third, *we can share our own personal experience with Jesus to others.* In Mark 5:19, after healing a demon-possessed man, Jesus said to him, "Go home to your people and report to them what great things the Lord has done for you, and how He had mercy on you." People can argue with various points of theology and Bible interpretation, but it's hard to argue with the evidence of a changed life.

Fourth, *we can let the Holy Spirit lead us.* Jesus said, "But the Helper, the Holy Spirit whom the Father will send in My name, He will teach you all things, and remind you of all that I said to you" (John 14:26). You can't prepare for every possible spiritual question people may throw at you, but you can prepare for the most common questions. You can also prepare yourself to answer people from different religions, because most of them ask similar questions. But most importantly, you need to seek the Holy Spirit's guidance as you share with others the most important answers they may ever receive.

——————————— DIG DEEP ———————————

You never know when someone will ask you a question of eternal importance. Be ready in and out of season to give a convincing explanation of the gospel. Ask yourself the following questions and answer them truthfully:

1. Which questions about faith and the Bible do you feel most comfortable answering, and which questions do you feel least comfortable answering?
2. Are you ready to share the gospel with a Hindu, a Muslim, a Buddhist, or an atheist? If not, why not?

One Way

Jesus said to him, "I am the way, and the truth, and the
life; no one comes to the Father except through Me."
—JOHN 14:6

SOME VERSES IN THE BIBLE ARE POPULAR FOR A REASON.
Take John 3:16, for example. Who isn't moved by the idea of a God
who loves us so much that He would sacrifice His own Son so that
we can live forever? Or take Jesus' promise to give rest to "all who
are weary and burdened" (Matthew 11:28). Who doesn't want relief
from the pressures of daily life? People gladly embrace these verses
because they make them feel good. Other verses, however, make
people uncomfortable. As a result, people tend to ignore them,
explain them away, or attack Christians who live by them.

God doesn't give us the option of choosing which Bible passages
to live by. Paul said, "All Scripture is inspired by God and beneficial
for teaching, for rebuke, for correction, for training in righteousness" (2 Timothy 3:16). *All Scripture.* If a part of Scripture offends us,
it means we need work on that area of our faith. The problem is not
with Scripture but with our perspective.

Proverbs 14:12 says, "There is a way which seems right to a man,
but its end is the way of death." One way that seems right to a lot of
people is inclusiveness, the idea that all belief systems are equally
valid. This makes everyone feel affirmed. It encourages people to be
open-minded. It resolves conflict between people who have different
spiritual views.

The problem is, inclusiveness is based on a lie. Jesus left no room for compromise or inclusiveness in John 14:6. He said, "I am the way." Sin created an enormous divide between us and God. There was nothing we could do on our own to cross that divide. God's holiness demanded that our sin be punished by death. Unless a perfect sacrifice was made by a sinless person, we had no hope of eternal life.

That left only one option, because only Jesus has lived a sinless life. Jesus conquered sin during His lifetime and conquered death after His crucifixion. No one else can offer eternal life. Paul said, "If Christ has not been raised, your faith is worthless; you are still in your sins" (1 Corinthians 15:17).

As tempting as it is to embrace the feel-good idea that there are different paths to God, we must recognize that if there is another way to eternal life, Jesus' death and resurrection were unnecessary. God the Father confirmed that there is no other way to salvation when Jesus asked Him, "If it is possible, let this cup pass from Me" (Matthew 26:39). There was no other way.

There is only one way to God: "Believe in the Lord Jesus, and you will be saved" (Acts 16:31).

DIG DEEP

People label Christians as narrow-minded for believing that Jesus is the only way to God. But if we truly love others, how can we not tell them the truth that can set them free? Ask yourself the following questions and answer them truthfully:

1. Why is Jesus the only way to the Father?
2. How would you respond to someone who was offended by your lack of inclusiveness?

Consider It All Joy

*Consider it all joy, my brethren, when you encounter various
trials, knowing that the testing of your faith produces
endurance. And let endurance have its perfect result, so
that you may be perfect and complete, lacking in nothing.*
—JAMES 1:2–4

"CONSIDER IT ALL JOY . . . WHEN YOU ENCOUNTER VARI-
ous trials." There's no way of knowing how the original recipients
of James's letter reacted when they read those first few words. It's
possible their reactions weren't much different from the reactions
of people today. *How are we supposed to find joy in the midst of financial difficulties? Or health issues? Or relationship problems? Or personal
failures?*

In other words, *How can we consider it all joy when there's nothing
joyful about our circumstances?* To answer that question, we first need
to look beyond our immediate circumstances to the bigger picture.
If we keep our focus narrow, we will see only the pain, anxiety, and
discomfort caused by the trials.

The wiser approach is to look at the big picture and ask, "What
good things can come from this bad situation?" That's what it means
to "consider it all joy": to recognize that God can do something
extraordinary in even the worst circumstances.

Joseph endured the trials of slavery in Egypt after his own brothers sold him. Years later, when he was reunited with his brothers, he
said, "As for you, you meant evil against me, but God meant it for
good in order to bring about this present result, to preserve many

people alive" (Genesis 50:20). Joseph could see the big picture. He understood that his trials put him in the right place, at the right time, with the right skills to accomplish God's will.

Second, *we need to consider whether God is disciplining us.* Some trials are the result of our own actions or poor decisions. And God, in His wisdom, allows us to suffer the consequences. He does it not out of spite but out of love. He wants us to learn from the experience so that we don't repeat it. Hebrews 12:11 says, "All discipline for the moment seems not to be joyful, but sorrowful; yet to those who have been trained by it, afterwards it yields the peaceful fruit of righteousness."

Third, *we need to embrace the end result*: "That you may be perfect and complete, lacking in nothing." "Perfect," in this context, doesn't mean "sinless" or "flawless"; it means "mature." Trials take us out of our comfort zone. They test our endurance. But if we consider it all joy when we experience them, they also deepen our relationship with God. They give us empathy for other people who are struggling. They make us more spiritually mature.

And that makes us more useful to God. Through trials we learn that we can never find true joy and peace from temporary things; joy and peace come only from God, even in the middle of a storm.

DIG DEEP

Trials are inevitable. The question is, will they rob you of your joy? Ask yourself the following questions and answer them truthfully:

1. What was the last major trial you faced?
2. What impact did it have on you at the time?
3. Looking at the big picture, what are some good things God accomplished through your trial?

The Difference Between Man-Made Religion and Christianity

"This people honors Me with their lips, but their heart is far away from Me. 'But in vain do they worship Me, teaching as doctrines the precepts of men.'"
—MATTHEW 15:8–9

YOU WOULD THINK THAT WHEN JESUS CAME TO EARTH, the religious leaders of Israel would have welcomed Him. After all, these men had spent their entire lives studying God's Word. From all appearances no one had a closer relationship with God than they did. They should have been overjoyed to greet His Son as the long-awaited Messiah.

But instead of embracing Jesus, most of them burned with hatred toward Him. They didn't just reject Him; they opposed Him at every turn. They challenged Him in public to try to make Him look foolish. They plotted against Him. They accused Him of being demon-possessed. They made plans to kill Him.

They considered Jesus a threat because He exposed them for what they were. These men loved religion, not God. They showed outward signs of having a relationship with God, but inwardly they were empty. They loved to follow rules because they believed it made them more righteous than everyone else. But Jesus showed everyone just how meaningless their religion was. These men were proud of their respected place in the community, but they had no real relationship with God. They missed the one thing that mattered the most.

Doing religious deeds through the sinful flesh is not only wrong but dangerous. Isaiah said, "All our righteous deeds are like a filthy garment" (Isaiah 64:6). Some religious leaders wanted to control their own eternal destinies. They wanted to be good enough, to obey enough rules, to earn God's favor. God's Word says that can't be done. "For by grace you have been saved through faith; and this is not of yourselves, it is the gift of God; not a result of works, so that no one may boast" (Ephesians 2:8–9).

Many people still confuse religion and Christianity today. They go to church and live respectable lives because that's what respectable people do. They obey commandments so that God will think they're good enough for heaven. But they have never been spiritually reborn. Jesus said, "Not everyone who says to Me, 'Lord, Lord,' will enter the kingdom of heaven, but the one who does the will of My Father who is in heaven will enter" (Matthew 7:21).

Religion says, "If you obey enough commandments, you can earn God's love and salvation. You can save yourself from hell." Jesus said, "If you love Me, you will keep My commandments" (John 14:15). Genuine obedience is driven by our love for Jesus, not by our confidence in our own goodness or our fear of hell.

People who put their faith in religion may enjoy a good reputation in their community or a sense of self-satisfaction. But those are surface rewards in this temporary world, while the real reward for this empty life is hell for all eternity. Spiritual death comes from false, man-made religion, while spiritual life comes from having a true relationship with God.

DIG DEEP

Paul said, "If anyone is in Christ, this person is a new creation" (2 Corinthians 5:17). Jesus—not religion—transforms us. Ask yourself the following questions and answer them truthfully:

1. What motivates you to obey God?
2. What inside-out changes has Jesus made in your life?

Fear God?

Let all the earth fear the Lord; let all the inhabitants
of the world stand in awe of Him.
—Psalm 33:8

SOME PEOPLE IN THE BIBLE HAD REASON TO BE AFRAID of God. Adam and Eve after they ate the fruit. The people of Sodom and Gomorrah. Jonah when he headed in the opposite direction of Nineveh.

But reborn Christians have no reason to be afraid of God, who Himself promised, "I will never desert you, nor will I ever abandon you" (Hebrews 13:5). Paul agreed: "For I am convinced that [nothing] will be able to separate us from the love of God, which is in Christ Jesus our Lord" (Romans 8:38–39).

Those promises fill us with comfort, not fear. So what does it mean to "fear the Lord"? The psalmist shed light on that question in the second half of Psalm 33:8: "Let all the inhabitants of the world stand in awe of Him." With God, the list of things to be awestruck about is endless. Every photo that astronomers get back from deep space sheds light on the enormity and beauty of His creation. Every answered prayer reveals His loving-kindness toward us.

The more we learn about God, the deeper our sense of awe-struck wonder grows. And the more we understand about His significance, the more our own insignificance comes into view. That was the reaction David had: "When I consider Your heavens, the work of Your fingers, the moon and the stars, which You have set in place; what is man that You take thought of him, and a son of man that You are concerned about him?" (Psalm 8:3–4).

The tension between celebrating our relationship with God and recognizing that we're not worthy of it helps us keep a healthy sense of awe. We need to understand who God is and accept certain truths about Him: He is sovereign, He is holy, He hates sin, He is just, He demands punishment for sin. We can't approach our relationship with God as we would any other relationship. We must show reverence for everything He is. We must also be vigilant not to do anything that would jeopardize our relationship with Him.

Solomon said, "The fear of the LORD is the beginning of knowledge" (Proverbs 1:7). If we stay mindful of our relationship with God, we will be more conscious of obeying Him. We will be more willing to learn from His discipline. We will worship Him in a way that's meaningful to Him and us. Not having an immense amount of respect for God might also be a sign of a false Christian, a lukewarm Christian whom God will spit out of His mouth (Revelation 3:16). Nothing but good can come from a healthy fear of God.

DIG DEEP

If you're a reborn Christian, you can rejoice that you have no reason to be afraid of God. Showing a proper fear, or awe, of Him will make a huge difference in your life. Ask yourself the following questions and answer them truthfully:

1. How might a healthy fear of God guide you in making decisions?
2. What might a healthy fear of God look like in your worship of Him?

Why Doesn't God Answer My Prayers?

A prayer of a righteous person, when it is
brought about, can accomplish much.
—JAMES 5:16

IF YOU'VE EVER FELT LIKE YOUR PRAYERS WEREN'T
being answered, you're in good company. David begged God to
spare the life of his child. Paul asked God to remove an affliction
that was making his life miserable. Moses, Job, Elijah, and Jonah all
prayed for God to take their lives. None of the things they prayed
for came to pass. God's Word has much to say about the unlimited
potential of prayer. But it also has much to say about why that potential is sometimes difficult to unleash.

The first reason is *sin*. Sin creates a wall between us and God.
Isaiah 59:1–2 says, "Behold, the LORD's hand is not so short that it
cannot save; nor is His ear so dull that it cannot hear. But your wrongdoings have caused a separation between you and your God, and your
sins have hidden His face from you so that He does not hear." If you
disobey God and don't ask Him for forgiveness, you have no reason to
expect Him to answer your prayers.

If you're not sure whether sin is affecting your prayers, ask God
to show you. If you are sure, confess. John said, "If we confess our
sins, He is faithful and righteous, so that He will forgive us our sins
and cleanse us from all unrighteousness" (1 John 1:9). Once sin is
confessed and forgiven, the lines of communication open up again.

The second reason our prayers might be hindered is that we are *praying against God's will*. James said, "You ask and do not receive, because you ask with wrong motives, so that you may spend what you request on your pleasures" (James 4:3). Not every opportunity is from God. We can't jump into something and then ask God to bless us. We need to first discover whether the opportunity is part of His will. God's will is to expand His kingdom—in our lives and in the world around us. That should be our motivation as we pray, instead of pursuing selfish goals such as material gain, comfort, or popularity.

The third reason is *not praying in faith*. James said, "But he must ask in faith without any doubting, for the one who doubts is like the surf of the sea, driven and tossed by the wind" (James 1:6). Some people find it hard to believe that God will do what He says He will do. So they get caught in a prayer loop. They keep praying for something, even if it's already been answered, because they find it hard to accept His answer. People struggling with guilt who haven't forgiven themselves—or who are still dealing with consequences from others—may keep praying for forgiveness. They don't understand that God forgives more readily than people do.

God is ready to do great things in and through you. The healthier your prayer life is, the more you will thrive in His will.

DIG DEEP

Jesus said, "If you remain in Me, and My words remain in you, ask whatever you wish, and it will be done for you" (John 15:7). The way to remain in the Lord is to always live through His Spirit in you and to spend time with Him, praying and listening. Ask yourself the following questions and answer them truthfully:

1. What is keeping you from unleashing the full potential of prayer?
2. How can you tell if something is God's will?
3. When should you stop praying for something?

So Much Pain

"These things I have spoken to you so that in Me you
may have peace. In the world you have tribulation,
but take courage; I have overcome the world."
—JOHN 16:33

WHEN WE EXPERIENCE PAIN AND SUFFERING, WE OFTEN
want to ask God, "Why did You let this happen?" But we won't always
have immediate answers. One of my brothers was shot to death.
Another died in a car crash. My father died after a painful battle with
multiple myeloma, a form of cancer. The answers in God's Word may
not always bring comfort right away, but they do bring understanding and spiritual growth. And that can help us persevere through
even the worst circumstances.

The first thing we need to understand is that *God has given us*
freedom of choice (or free will). John said, "Beloved, let us love one
another" (1 John 4:7). God could have forced us to love one another,
but how meaningful would that have been? Instead, He put the decision in our hands.

Sadly, many people choose not to love. In many cases they
choose to pursue evil, and their wrong choices cause suffering and
pain. Take my brother's killer, for example. His evil decision caused
my family and friends years of deep pain and suffering. Entire popu-
lations face starvation because of both greed—through the unequal
distribution of resources, and hatred—through civil war. We could
ask God to intervene, but then we would be asking Him to take away
our freedom of choice.

The truth is, He does intervene at times with our free will intact. Look at how God stopped Paul, at the time called Saul, from persecuting Christians. His angels are still ministering spirits to us today (Hebrews 1:14). You probably have no idea how many times God has saved you from something.

The second thing we need to understand is that *suffering can bring us closer to God*. The loss of my brothers opened my spiritual eyes to accept Jesus as my Lord and Savior. It also made me appreciate my remaining brother and sister so much more. Sometimes God allows suffering in our lives to show us our need for Him. The brokenness of the world motivates us to turn to the One who heals and restores and provides peace and comfort.

James said, "Every good thing given and every perfect gift is from above, coming down from the Father of lights, with whom there is no variation or shifting shadow" (James 1:17). Those good and perfect gifts restore our lives and give us the strength to persevere.

The third thing we need to understand is *the hope we have in heaven*. This world and the things of this world, including the suffering we experience, cannot even begin to compare to the eternal glory that awaits those who have run the race until the end (Romans 8:18).

DIG DEEP

God promises that in heaven there will be no more pain or suffering. So you need to persevere only for a short time. Ask yourself the following questions and answer them truthfully:

1. When was the last time you questioned why God allowed something to happen?
2. How has God made His good and perfect gifts known to you in your suffering?

God in the Flesh

*Christ Jesus . . . emptied Himself by taking the form of a
bond-servant and being born in the likeness of men. And
being found in appearance as a man, He humbled Himself by
becoming obedient to the point of death: death on a cross.*
—Philippians 2:5–8

JESUS' SACRIFICE DIDN'T BEGIN AT THE CROSS. IT BEGAN
the moment He took human form. Remember, Jesus is God. He
spoke the universe into existence. He breathed life into us. There
is no limit to His knowledge and power. Yet He laid those things
aside to come to earth as a baby and dwell among His creation.
He left His perfect existence in heaven for a life of rejection on
our sin-filled planet. He made Himself vulnerable to pain, sickness,
exhaustion, and death. He squeezed His infinite presence into a
human body.

Imagine the agony that transition caused Him. Imagine the love
that motivated His sacrifice. There was no other option. The Bible
makes that quite clear. Paul explained in Romans 5:18–19: "So then,
as through one offense the result was condemnation to all mankind,
so also through one act of righteousness the result was justification
of life to all mankind. For as through the one man's disobedience the
many were made sinners, so also through the obedience of the One
the many will be made righteous." Adam, the first man, brought sin
into the world with his disobedience, creating a separation between
God and humans. God's holiness and justice demand eternal punishment for sin. The only way for our relationship to be restored

was for another human to do what Adam could not: live a perfectly obedient life.

No normal human being could do it, so God Himself came to earth in human form to live a sinless life and then give His life as a sacrifice. This is His perfect plan of redemption. One man's disobedience made us unrighteous; one Man's obedience makes us righteous again. This is why Paul called Jesus "the last Adam" (1 Corinthians 15:45) and "the second man" (verse 47). If Jesus had not come in human flesh, He couldn't have paid the price for our sins.

During His time on earth, Jesus experienced everything we experience. He faced temptation, pain, and rejection. He knew what it was like to be hungry and tired. He felt righteous anger. He laughed. He cried. All this makes Him the perfect Adviser and Counselor to turn to with our own experiences. Hebrews 2:18 says, "For since He Himself was tempted in that which He has suffered, He is able to come to the aid of those who are tempted."

Jesus also gave us an example to follow in how to please God. John said, "the one who says he remains in [Jesus] ought, himself also, walk just as He walked" (1 John 2:6). No matter what situation we face, we can find the guidance we need by asking one question: What would Jesus do?

DIG DEEP

You may never understand the depth of Jesus' sacrifice in taking on human form. But you can spend your life trying to learn more about Him and live as He did. Ask yourself the following questions and answer them truthfully:

1. What are you currently dealing with that Jesus would understand?
2. What is your biggest challenge right now in trying to live as Jesus did?

What Is Heaven Like?

But just as it is written: "Things which eye has not seen and ear has not heard, and which have not entered the heart of man, all that God has prepared for those who love Him."
—1 CORINTHIANS 2:9

BEFORE YOU MOVE TO A NEW PLACE, YOU WANT TO FIND out as much as you can about it. When that place is heaven, gathering information is especially important, as that's where reborn believers will spend eternity.

Understanding what heaven is like can be challenging because only a few people have been given a glimpse of heaven before they died. And those who did get a glimpse were overwhelmed. Their descriptions are beyond anything we could possibly imagine, but we can put together some important clues by reading Scripture.

First, in heaven *our perspective will be transformed.* Paul said, "For now we see in a mirror dimly, but then face to face; now I know in part, but then I will know fully, just as I also have been fully known" (1 Corinthians 13:12). In this verse the Greek word *epiginosko* means "to really know" or "to know extensively." In heaven our questions will be answered. We will understand God and His work more clearly. We will experience all that He has to offer more intensely.

Second, in heaven *we will work.* If you were counting on an eternal heavenly retirement, that may not seem like good news. But consider this: God created us to enjoy work—to find purpose, meaning, satisfaction, and fulfillment in our labors. In the perfect environment of the garden of Eden, Adam and Eve were caretakers. Doing their important work intensified their enjoyment of paradise.

Their sin, and the curse that came with it, changed things completely (Genesis 3:17). Work became difficult—a source of drudgery, not fulfillment. In heaven the original order will be restored. Revelation 22:3 says, "There will no longer be any curse; and the throne of God and of the Lamb will be in it, and His bond-servants will serve Him." We will serve. We will work. And it will be amazing.

Third, in heaven *we will be reunited with loved ones who are reborn believers*. Paul wrote these words to believers who were mourning the loss of a loved one: "For the Lord Himself will descend from heaven with a shout, with the voice of the archangel and with the trumpet of God, and the dead in Christ will rise first. Then we who are alive, who remain, will be caught up together with them in the clouds to meet the Lord in the air, and so we shall always be with the Lord. Therefore comfort one another with these words" (1 Thessalonians 4:16–18).

That last sentence is the key. The reason to learn all we can about heaven is so that we can comfort one another with what we know. We can encourage one another to keep our eyes on Jesus and to run the race until the end.

DIG DEEP

Life in this world can be tough. Knowing that we have someplace amazing to look forward to gives us motivation to persevere. Ask yourself the following questions and answer them truthfully:

1. What do you look forward to learning when you will understand things more fully in heaven?
2. Are you and your family using the time you have in this temporary world to prepare for heaven?

The Power of Empathy

Jesus wept.
—John 11:35

THE SCENE WAS SET FOR ONE OF JESUS' MOST AMAZING miracles. He had received word that His friend Lazarus was on his deathbed. Instead of hurrying to say goodbye—or, better yet, heal him—Jesus stayed where He was for two days. By the time He finally got to Lazarus's hometown of Bethany, Lazarus was dead. Just as Jesus knew he would be. The reason Jesus didn't rush to Lazarus's bedside is that He had another plan in mind. He wanted to show His power over death itself.

Friends and loved ones were deep into their mourning when Jesus arrived. Lazarus's sister Mary came to greet Him. Through her tears, she said, "Lord, if You had been here, my brother would not have died" (John 11:32).

The Lord's response is an amazing snapshot of empathy. "Therefore when Jesus saw her weeping, and the Jews who came with her also weeping, He was deeply moved in spirit and was troubled" (verse 33). Jesus noticed. He had come to Bethany to perform an awesome, life-changing task. But He didn't allow Himself to become task-oriented. He knew that the people's sadness would soon turn to joy. But He didn't discount their sadness. Instead, Jesus felt every bit of it. His love for people was so powerful that He couldn't overlook their pain, even for a moment.

So Jesus wept. He didn't try to talk them out of their emotions. He cried with them. Ecclesiastes 3:1 says, "There is an appointed time for everything. And there is a time for every matter under heaven." The time to raise Lazarus from the dead was coming. But at that moment, it was time to mourn with those who loved him.

Certainly no one who was at Lazarus's tomb that day ever forgot the sight of him walking out, still wrapped in his burial clothes. But the people paying close attention that day likely also never forgot the sight of Jesus crying with them. Not only did He have the power to raise people from the dead but He also had the ability—and the willingness—to feel what they were feeling.

Psalm 147:3 says, "He heals the brokenhearted and binds up their wounds." The promise of healing gives us comfort. But notice that before the Lord heals us, He recognizes us as being brokenhearted and knows what's going on deep in our hearts. He senses our pain and the cause of it. He understands its impact in our lives. He feels it. He hurts for us and He hurts with us.

In doing so, Jesus sets a powerful example for reborn believers. We can make a profound difference in the lives of others by empathizing with their pain and struggles. And while we may be limited to providing comfort and encouragement, we can point the way to the One who offers genuine healing.

DIG DEEP

The takeaway from this story comes from Peter, who was there that day. He instructed believers to "humble yourselves under the mighty hand of God, . . . having cast all your anxiety on Him, because He cares for you" (1 Peter 5:6–7). Ask yourself the following questions and answer them truthfully:

1. What does it mean to you that Jesus feels your pain?
2. Are you sometimes too task-orientated to see what people are feeling?
3. How can you learn from Jesus and empathize with someone who is hurting?

The Difference Between Jesus and Other Religious Leaders

And the Word became flesh, and dwelt among us;
and we saw His glory, glory as of the only Son
from the Father, full of grace and truth.
—JOHN 1:14

SOME PEOPLE RESPECTFULLY REFER TO JESUS AS A "great religious leader." They recognize the impact that Christianity has had on the world, but they see it as just one of several major religions. And they lump Jesus together with the Buddha, Muhammad, and other founders of major religions.

But Jesus is not like any other religious leader. In fact, His uniqueness is at the center of our Christian beliefs. The Bible offers several examples of what sets Jesus apart. First, *Jesus showed His power over nature*. Luke 8 tells the story of a sea journey that turned dangerous when a storm threatened to sink the boat that Jesus and His disciples were on. Jesus "rebuked the wind and the surging waves, and they stopped, and it became calm" (verse 24).

The disciples' reaction speaks volumes. "They were fearful and amazed, saying to one another, 'Who then is this, that He commands even the winds and the water, and they obey Him?'" (verse 25). The answer is simple: He is the Creator. He spoke the universe into existence, so it should be no surprise that He has complete control over it. His power overrides the laws of physics.

Second, *Jesus fulfilled roughly three hundred Old Testament prophecies when He came*, so there was no question of who He was and what He intended to do. Hundreds of years before Jesus was born, Old Testament prophets told people how they would recognize the Messiah, God's Son, when He came. Isaiah predicted that He would be born of a virgin (Isaiah 7:14). Micah announced that He would come from Bethlehem (Micah 5:2). Isaiah also prophesied that Jesus would be crucified (Isaiah 53:4–5) at a time when crucifixion did not even exist. Jesus fulfilled all these prophecies and hundreds more. He proved Himself to be our Messiah, Savior, and Lord.

Third, *Jesus conquered death.* Siddhartha Gautama, or the Buddha, as he is known today, died in the fourth century BC after eating pork that may have been spoiled. His body was cremated. Muhammad died in Medina on June 8, 632 CE, after a brief illness. He was buried in a mosque. The religions these men founded lived on, but they did not. The same goes for all the other founders of major religions. Except one.

Jesus gave His life on the cross to satisfy God's holiness and justice. His death paid the price for the sins of the world, but death was not the end. Three days later, He rose again. More than five hundred people saw Him at one time. After forty more days on earth, Jesus ascended to heaven, where He lives today. Only Jesus had the power to conquer death itself.

These three examples barely scratch the surface when it comes to Jesus' uniqueness. But they help us understand that He is not just another great religious leader. And Christianity is not just another religion.

DIG DEEP

Jesus didn't just start a religion. He bridged the gap between you and God and made eternal life possible. Ask yourself the following questions and answer them truthfully:

1. What would you say to someone who referred to Jesus as a great religious leader?
2. How is Christianity different from other religions?

What Will Happen at the Rapture?

Behold, I tell you a mystery; we will not all sleep, but we will all be changed, in a moment, in the twinkling of an eye, at the last trumpet; for the trumpet will sound, and the dead will be raised imperishable, and we will be changed.
—1 Corinthians 15:51–52

WHILE JESUS' DISCIPLES WATCHED HIM ASCEND INTO heaven, two men (who were probably angels) asked them, "Why do you stand looking into the sky? This Jesus, who has been taken up from you into heaven, will come in the same way as you have watched Him go into heaven" (Acts 1:11). Since that time, Christians have been looking forward to Jesus' reappearance, which is known as the rapture.

The word "rapture" isn't in the Bible. It comes from the Greek word *harpazo*, which means "caught up." Paul referred to it when he said, "Then we who are alive, who remain, will be caught up together with them in the clouds to meet the Lord in the air, and so we will always be with the Lord" (1 Thessalonians 4:17). Reborn believers who are alive when Jesus descends from heaven will be "caught up" to meet Jesus. From that moment on, we will always be with Him.

This event is different from Jesus' second coming, when He will return to earth to conquer His enemies and establish His kingdom. As Paul explained in 1 Corinthians 15, when the rapture occurs, the bodies of believers who are alive will be immediately transformed into eternal bodies. From an earthly perspective, they will suddenly vanish.

When all reborn Christians are gone, God will pour out His judgment on the earth. This event is known as the tribulation. Jesus described it this way: "For then there will be a great tribulation, such as has not occurred since the beginning of the world until now, nor ever will again" (Matthew 24:21).

Some Christians believe the rapture will occur before the tribulation, others believe it will happen in the middle, and others believe it will happen at the end. I believe that Jesus' promise to us in John 14:3—"If I go and prepare a place for you, I am coming again and will take you to Myself, so that where I am, there you also will be"— refers to the rapture. We will be with Jesus while the events of the tribulation take place.

Whatever our beliefs about the rapture, however, we must not let our differences come between us. Paul warned believers to stop quarreling over opinions (Romans 14:1). The devil knows how to turn minor quarrels into major divisions. His goal is to distract us from our common purpose. Paul said, "We are ambassadors for Christ" (2 Corinthians 5:20). This world is not our home. But as ambassadors, we have a job to do. We must help as many people as we can to escape God's wrath by sharing the gospel with them. We must increase the number of people who will be caught up with us when the rapture occurs.

DIG DEEP

No matter what anyone tells you, you cannot predict when the rapture will occur or the date of your death. All you can do is live every day as if it is your last. Ask yourself the following questions and answer them truthfully:

1. What are your biggest concerns about the rapture?
2. Why is it important to know what the Bible describes about the future?

Understanding God's Commandments

"If you love Me, you will keep My commandments."
—JOHN 14:15

HUMAN NATURE IS A STRANGE THING. WHEN WE'RE given a set of rules, many people's first instinct is to look for ways to get around those rules. We assume they work against our best interests because they restrict our freedom.

God's commandments teach us right from wrong. They show us how holy and just He is. Paul said, "The Law is holy, and the commandment is holy and righteous and good" (Romans 7:12). They show us that it is impossible to save ourselves by obeying His law. This is why we can only be saved through faith and not by works, but our works prove that our faith is real. God's law shines the light on darkness, on the evil within the world, and on the consequences of sin. Sin leads only to pain, suffering, and death. The evil, sinful nature within humans is a sickness that we cannot cure ourselves. God is the only cure. Only He can set us free from the hold that sin has over us.

In the Old Testament, Israel had over six hundred laws to follow. The New Testament shows believers that the commandments are not just about our outward actions; they also apply to our intentions. Jesus said, "You have heard that it was said, 'You shall not commit adultery'; but I say to you that everyone who looks at a woman with lust for her has already committed adultery with her in his heart" (Matthew 5:27–28).

Is it possible to obey God's commandments when all of us have fallen short of His glory (Romans 3:23)? Yes, through Christ "all things are possible" (Mark 9:23). When we accept Christ as Lord and Savior, He declares us as righteous and puts His Spirit inside us. The Spirit then gives us the power to overcome sin, but we must choose to be led by the Spirit. Paul said, "But I say, walk by the Spirit, and you will not carry out the desire of the flesh. For the desire of the flesh is against the Spirit, and the Spirit against the flesh; for these are in opposition to one another, in order to keep you from doing whatever you want. But if you are led by the Spirit, you are not under the Law" (Galatians 5:16–18).

Through the power of the Spirit, God helps us to live our best lives, free from the ugly consequences of sin. If you are a true child of God, you will want to please God and obey His commandments because you love Him. You have His Spirit in you and can therefore produce the fruit of the Spirit and overcome sin in your life.

DIG DEEP

When Jesus was asked about the greatest commandment, He said, "'You shall love the LORD your God with all your heart, and with all your soul, and with all your mind.' This is the great and foremost commandment. The second is like it, 'You shall love your neighbor as yourself'" (Matthew 22:37–39). Ask yourself the following questions and answer them truthfully:

1. How do these two commandments get to the heart of God's law?
2. Paul wrote, "The law of the Spirit of life in Christ Jesus has set you free from the law of sin and of death" (Romans 8:2). What does this mean?
3. What sin in your life do you need to overcome?

◆ DAY 41 ◆

Born Again?

Nicodemus said to Him, "How can a person be born
when he is old? He cannot enter a second time into
his mother's womb and be born, can he?"
—JOHN 3:4

NOT ALL JEWISH RELIGIOUS LEADERS IN JESUS' DAY
opposed Him. A few were able to humbly admit that He taught the
truth and His miracles were signs from God. One of them, a man
named Nicodemus, even met privately with Jesus to learn more. Of
course, he did it at night, when no one else would see him. Being seen
with Jesus would have ruined his reputation.

Jesus got right to the point. "Truly, truly, I say to you, unless
someone is born again he cannot see the kingdom of God" (John
3:3). Our salvation depends on being born again. But what does that
mean? The concept confused Nicodemus, and it confuses a lot of
people today.

God is Spirit, and when we are born from God, we become spiritually alive. The phrase "born again" literally means "born from above"
or "born from God." John shed some light on it when he wrote, "No
one who has been born of God practices sin, because His seed remains
in him; and he cannot sin continually, because he has been born of
God" (1 John 3:9). He is talking about a complete transformation. This
is the same transformation Paul talked about in 2 Corinthians 5:17:
"Therefore if anyone is in Christ, this person is a new creature; the old
things passed away; behold, new things have come."

The transformation, or the act of being born again, begins with

God revealing His truth to us. Paul said, "But a natural man does not accept the things of the Spirit of God, for they are foolishness to him, and he cannot understand them, because they are spiritually appraised" (1 Corinthians 2:14). He helps us understand who He is, what Jesus did, and why we need to be saved. He shows us how meaningless life is without Him. That meaninglessness explains why so many people are unhappy and empty. They try to fill the emptiness with relationships, money, traveling, eating, drinking, drugs, porn, and other things, but they can never be satisfied with material things. What they really yearn for is a new spiritual life. And only God can give that.

If we respond to God's truth, ask forgiveness for our sins, and accept Christ as our Lord and Savior, we are born again. Peter said, "Blessed be the God and Father of our Lord Jesus Christ, who according to His great mercy has caused us to be born again to a living hope through the resurrection of Jesus Christ from the dead" (1 Peter 1:3). We find new meaning, new purpose, and new fulfillment.

When we are born again, we receive eternal life and the Holy Spirit comes to live inside us and seals us until the day of redemption. He also changes the way we think, speak, and act. We receive the power to overcome sin and the freedom to live as God intends us to with that peace that surpasses all understanding. That's what it means to be born again.

DIG DEEP

Being born again changes everything. Ask yourself the following questions and answer them truthfully:

1. Have you been born again? If so, how would you explain the transformation that occurred?
2. What does living as God intends look like in your life?

Should I Fast?

So we fasted and sought our God concerning this
matter, and He listened to our pleading.
—EZRA 8:23

DAVID FASTED FOR SEVEN DAYS AS HE PRAYED FOR GOD
to spare the life of his son (2 Samuel 12:1–23). Moses fasted before
he climbed the mountain to receive God's commandments
(Deuteronomy 9:9–18). Ezra fasted as part of his mourning over the
sins of the Jewish people while they were in captivity (Ezra 10:6–17).
Daniel fasted as he waited for God to reveal the meaning of a vision
(Daniel 10:1–3). Jesus fasted for forty days while He prepared to face
Satan's temptations in the wilderness (Matthew 4:1–2).

In Scripture, fasting is connected to prayer. It's a way of focusing
intently on God's will by giving up something important for a period
of time. Fasting is a way of showing God that we're serious about our
prayer—or that we're committed to seeking His face. What better
way to show our commitment than to sacrifice worldly things so
we can draw closer to God? The more we sacrifice, the more we
gain. James said, "Come close to God and He will come close to you"
(James 4:8).

But fasting isn't something to enter into lightly. First, *you need
to decide what kind of fast you want to do.* You can do a short fast by
abstaining from something for six to twenty-four hours. You can do
an intermittent fast, where you fast for, say, sixteen hours every day
for a period of time. You can do a "Daniel fast" (named after the Old
Testament prophet, not me), where you abstain from eating certain

things for twenty-one days. For example, you might eat only plant-based foods and drink only water.

Second, *you'll need to decide what you want to give up for your fast.* Food is the obvious choice, of course. But for some people, giving up food altogether isn't an option. So you may choose instead to give up specific foods—such as junk food, meat, sweets, or coffee. Or you may choose to give up something other than food, such as social media, television, music, or hobbies. The key is to sacrifice something important to you.

Third, *you'll need to embrace a God-honoring attitude toward your fast.* Jesus warned, "Now whenever you fast, do not make a gloomy face as the hypocrites do, for they distort their faces so that they will be noticed by people when they are fasting. Truly I say to you, they have their reward in full. But as for you, when you fast, anoint your head and wash your face, so that your fasting will not be noticed by people but by your Father who is in secret; and your Father who sees what is done in secret will reward you" (Matthew 6:16–18). If you try to draw attention to yourself, you're missing the point.

DIG DEEP

Fasting is one of the most intensely personal things you can do—something that's between only you and God. It can energize your spiritual life and deepen your relationship with Him in amazing ways. Ask yourself the following questions and answer them truthfully:

1. When was the last time you fasted?
2. What do you want to accomplish through fasting?
3. What will you sacrifice to draw closer to God?

What Is Hell Like?

"And if your hand causes you to sin, cut it off; it is better
for you to enter life maimed, than, having your two
hands, to go into hell, into the unquenchable fire."
—MARK 9:43

JESUS SAID, "FOR GOD SO LOVED THE WORLD, THAT HE gave His only Son, so that everyone who believes in Him shall not perish, but have eternal life" (John 3:16). But what about the people who reject God's gift of salvation?

Some argue that nothing bad will happen, that God will ultimately take pity on them and allow them into heaven with those who believe. But that's not what Jesus said. And only He is the Source of truth.

John began his gospel with these words: "In the beginning was the Word, and the Word was with God, and the Word was God" (John 1:1). Later in that same chapter he wrote, "And the Word became flesh, and dwelt among us, and we saw His glory, glory as of the only Son from the Father, full of grace and truth" (verse 14). Our Christian faith is built on the truth of what Jesus said, not on what we would like to believe.

Here's what Jesus said about hell: "Depart from Me, you accursed people, into the eternal fire which has been prepared for the devil and his angels" (Matthew 25:41). The words "depart from Me" help us see that hell is a banishment from the Lord's presence. That alone is unimaginably horrific. After all, everything that is good comes from God. James put it this way: "Every good thing given and every perfect gift is from above, coming down from the Father of lights, with whom there is no variation or shifting shadow" (James 1:17). Hell is the complete absence of everything good, everything that makes life enjoyable—or even bearable.

Notice also that James referred to God as the "Father of lights." John added that "this is the message we have heard from Him and announce to you, that God is Light, and in Him there is no darkness at all" (1 John 1:5). God is light, so to be banished from His presence is to be deprived of all light. Hell is total darkness. Jesus also described hell as an "eternal fire." It's not just the absence of light; hell is a place of real suffering. The fire of hell burns, but it doesn't consume. So the agony it causes never ends. Hell is a place of eternal torment.

God is the perfect judge of the world, and hell is the punishment for sins. This shows us how holy God is and how evil our sins really are. But no one has to experience hell, because Jesus already took the punishment for our sins on the cross. God's gift of eternal life—amazing, joyous eternal life—is for everyone. All we have to do is accept it.

—————————— DIG DEEP ——————————

Hell is often portrayed as a "party place," while heaven is portrayed as boring. As a result, many unbelievers have a dangerously confused attitude about eternity. Ask yourself the following questions and answer them truthfully:

1. What misconceptions about hell have you encountered?
2. Why is it hard for some people to accept the reality of hell?
3. How can you help people understand what's at stake when it comes to accepting Christ as Savior and Lord?

When God Turned His Back

"My God, My God, why have You forsaken Me?"
—MATTHEW 27:46

PEOPLE USE THE WORD "GODFORSAKEN" TO DESCRIBE desolate places. But the reality of the word is far more devastating than we can possibly imagine.

Jesus experienced what it was to be God-forsaken during His crucifixion. In fact, He dreaded it hours earlier when He was with His disciples in the garden of Gethsemane just before His arrest. That's why He prayed, "My Father, if it is possible, let this cup pass from Me; yet not as I will, but as You will" (Matthew 26:39). The thought of having His heavenly Father turn against Him was almost too much for Jesus to bear. After all, He had been eternally with God the Father. He wanted to know for certain that His death was the only way to accomplish the Father's plan.

When the time finally came, and Jesus felt the full weight of His Father's abandonment, He spoke the words in Matthew 27 quoted above. To fully appreciate their meaning, we need to understand three things.

First, *Jesus was quoting Scripture*—Psalm 22:1, in fact. The words were written hundreds of years before Jesus came to earth as a human being. They refer to the Messiah, the Savior whom God promised would deliver His people. Jesus spoke the words to fulfill Old Testament prophecy and to show that He is the Messiah and Savior.

Second, *the spiritual and emotional pain Jesus experienced were far worse than His physical pain.* The gospel writers made no mention of

Jesus crying out when the soldiers beat Him or nailed His hands and feet to the cross. He suffered in silence as the pressure of His internal organs made it difficult to breathe. But when the full weight of the world's sins was placed on Him, He cried out in anguish.

The love Jesus had felt from His Father for eternity suddenly changed to wrath—God's righteous wrath against evil, against all sin. Jesus suffered the punishment for every sin ever committed. He experienced the full brunt of God's righteous judgment, and it was almost more than He could bear. After all, He Himself was sinless. Paul said, "[God] made Him who knew no sin to be sin on our behalf, so that we might become the righteousness of God in Him" (2 Corinthians 5:21).

And that brings us to the third point. *Jesus endured being forsaken by God the Father so that we will never have to.* Isaiah explained it this way: "But He was pierced through for our offenses, He was crushed for our wrongdoings; the punishment for our well-being was laid upon Him, and by His wounds we are healed" (Isaiah 53:5). We cannot repay Jesus for the sacrifice He made. But we can accept His gift of salvation and help others accept it too.

DIG DEEP

God will never turn His back on you. Jesus took the punishment for your sin so that you can have a loving relationship with the heavenly Father forever. Ask yourself the following questions and answer them truthfully:

1. Why does it sometimes feel as though God has abandoned you?
2. What can you do when you start to feel that way?
3. How can you help others who are struggling with feeling abandoned by God?

Water into Wine

This beginning of His signs Jesus did in Cana of Galilee,
and revealed His glory, and His disciples believed in Him.
—JOHN 2:11

JOHN ENDED HIS GOSPEL WITH AN AMAZING ADMISSION: "But there are also many other things which Jesus did, which, if they were written in detail, I expect that even the world itself would not contain the books that would be written" (John 21:25). One of the things John did write down was the first known miracle of Jesus, and it reveals some important truths.

The setting was a wedding celebration in Cana. Jesus attended, along with Mary (His mother) and His disciples. In the middle of the celebration (which lasted for days, as was the custom), the host ran out of wine. Mary, who may have been related to the host, turned to Jesus for help. In their brief interaction we see four things about Jesus that give us a deeper understanding of Him and His work.

First, *Jesus wanted to show His glory to His disciples so they would believe in Him.* We see this clearly in John 2:11: "This beginning of His signs Jesus did in Cana of Galilee, and revealed His glory; and His disciples believed in Him."

Second, *He honored His mother.* Mary knew that Jesus was the Messiah, the Son of God. She had known for thirty years, ever since the angel Gabriel told her that she was pregnant (Luke 1:26–35). But few other people knew. That's what Jesus was talking about when He said, "My hour has not yet come" (John 2:4). He had not yet revealed His power publicly. But that was about to change.

The fact that Mary went to Jesus when she learned about the wine shortage shows the faith and confidence she had in Him. She had no idea how Jesus would solve the problem, but she knew He was the person to turn to. That's why she said to the servants, "Whatever He tells you, do it" (John 2:5). For His part, Jesus saw His mother trying to help other people and determined to help her. He rewarded her faith and confidence by doing something unexpected. Something extraordinary. Something miraculous.

The third thing we notice about Jesus is that *He felt compassion*. In the culture of His day, hospitality was crucial. Running out of wine during a wedding celebration would have meant public humiliation for the hosts. Jesus empathized with their situation. So even though the circumstance wasn't a matter of life and death, or even someone's physical health, it still mattered to Jesus.

Fourth, *Jesus showed that He has power over nature*. He didn't turn grape juice into wine, so it wasn't just a matter of speeding up the fermentation process. He transformed water at a molecular level. He turned one substance into something it never would have otherwise become. He did it instantly, He did it on a large scale, and He did it in full view of witnesses.

In the three years that followed this incident, Jesus showed His power over nature in much more dramatic ways. But it was at the wedding in Cana where He first caused a select group of people to rethink their definition of "impossible."

DIG DEEP

Jesus can make good things happen in situations that seem hopeless—and He often does so in unexpected ways. Ask yourself the following questions and answer them truthfully:

1. What should you do when you face a situation that seems hopeless?
2. How has Jesus worked in unexpected ways in your life?

A Prayer for Forgiveness

For You, Lord, are good, and ready to forgive, and
abundant in mercy to all who call upon You.
—PSALM 86:5

EVERYONE NEEDS FORGIVENESS. PAUL SAID, "ALL HAVE sinned and fall short of the glory of God" (Romans 3:23). But not everyone knows how to ask for it. If you fall into that category, here's a prayer you can use to guide you.

Lord, I know that You are holy. And because I am Your child, You want me to be holy too. But I feel the sting of Paul's words in Romans 3:12: "There is no one who does good, there is not even one." This verse breaks all my excuses and attempts of trying to be good on my own, because I'm not good and I never will be in this world.

When I think about Your perfect holiness, I am overwhelmed with thankfulness for Your sacrifice. You are perfect, yet You took my sins on Yourself and died in my place. And there are so many sins for You to take on. Lord, I am so sorry. Please forgive me. You have forgiven my sins in the past, and here I am again. I gave in to temptation. I chose to do the wrong thing.

Lord, please forgive me. Wash me clean so that I will be as white as snow. Give me the power to walk in the Spirit, because I know Your Word says in Galatians 5:16–17, "But I say, walk by the Spirit, and you will not carry out the desire of the flesh. For the desire of the flesh is against the Spirit, and the Spirit against the flesh; for these are in opposition to one another, in order to keep you from doing whatever you want."

Lord, I'm struggling. Please help me to grow stronger spiritually so that I can overcome sin. Father, search my heart and take everything out that is not pleasing to You. Change me into the person You want me to be; my true identity is in You.

My Creator, my God, my Father, thank You that You love me, that You are a personal God, and that You listen to my prayers. As my Father, You always understand me, even when I'm not sure what to say.

I will keep fighting the daily battle against this evil nature within me. Thank You for Your grace because I cannot fight without it. Thank You that You are faithful and just, and that You have forgiven me. I can stand on Your Word and Your truth, which say I am forgiven.

Thank You, Lord, for Your kindness and understanding. Continue to change me from the inside out. Give me the strength and endurance to finish the fight. I will put on Your armor, and I will do battle again today. I will try my best to walk in the Spirit so that I will not fall into sin.

I trust You, my Lord, my Savior, my Father. Amen.

DIG DEEP

Forgiveness is one of God's greatest gifts. And it's available anytime to anyone who sincerely asks for it. Ask yourself the following questions and answer them truthfully:

1. Why is it dangerous not to ask God for forgiveness?
2. Is there any sin between you and God that you have not asked forgiveness for?
3. What would you say to someone who has trouble forgiving themself?

DAY 47 ◆

A Prayer for Protection

"These things I have spoken to you so that in Me you may have peace. In the world you have tribulation, but take courage; I have overcome the world."
—JOHN 16:33

GOD OFFERS AN AMAZING PROMISE IN ISAIAH 41:10: "DO not fear, for I am with you; do not be afraid, for I am your God. I will strengthen you, I will also help you, I will also uphold you with My righteous right hand." The day you became a reborn Christian is the day you also entered spiritual warfare, whether you like it or not. You will need God's help, and His protection is always just a prayer away. If you're not sure how to pray for His protection, here's a prayer to guide you.

Father, I humbly ask You to protect me from all forms of evil. Certain things are out of my control, and I fear what might happen. I fear for myself and I fear for my loved ones.

Forgive me for being afraid, because I know Your Word says that You have given me a spirit not of fear but of power, love, and self-control. This world—with all its problems, pain, and darkness—feels overwhelming at times, as though it's too powerful for me to handle. But You are so much bigger than this world. And he who dwells in the shelter of the Most High will abide in the shadow of the Almighty. You, Lord, are my refuge and fortress, my God, in whom I

106

trust. You are my hiding place and my shield. I have full hope in Your Scripture because every word proves true.

I know there are people doing evil things in this world, and that behind all evil lurks the devil. He prowls like a roaring lion seeking someone to devour. But Your Word gives me the power and authority to fight back. James 4:7 says, "Submit therefore to God. But resist the devil, and he will flee from you." It doesn't say he *might* flee. It says he *will* flee.

Father, I submit my whole life to You. I fully surrender every aspect of it to Your control. Help me to be sober-minded and watchful. Empower me with Your Spirit to overcome evil and shine Your light on darkness. Thank You for caring about me enough to protect me. You are Yahweh Nissi, the Lord my banner. I will not be shaken. I can say with confidence that the Lord is my helper, and I will not fear. What can people do to me? If God is for me, who can be against me? Even if I lose everything, then so be it. This world is not my home; it is only temporary. My home is with You, Lord. Even though I walk through the valley of the shadow of death, I will fear no evil, for You are with me. I will dwell in the house of the Lord forever. Amen.

DIG DEEP

Paul said, "But the Lord is faithful, and He will strengthen and protect you from the evil one" (2 Thessalonians 3:3). Ask yourself the following questions and answer them truthfully:

1. What evidence of the Lord's faithfulness have you seen, and in what areas do you need the Lord's protection right now?
2. Do you truly trust in God's promises when you have stress or anxiety? If not, why don't you?

The Dangers of Laziness

Be devoted to one another in brotherly love; give
preference to one another in honor; not lagging behind
in diligence, fervent in spirit, serving the Lord.
—ROMANS 12:10–11

SOMEONE ONCE SAID, "THE ONLY THING NECESSARY FOR
the triumph of evil is for good men to do nothing." Often the reason good men do nothing is because of spiritual apathy or laziness.
This type of laziness—or slothfulness—creates a vacuum for evil
to fill.

The Greek word translated as "laziness" in the Bible is *akēdia*,
which means "the absence of care." This kind of laziness isn't caused
by a lack of physical energy. It's a sinful condition of the heart that
causes people not to care about anyone or anything.

The consequences of laziness are dramatic. Proverbs 21:25 says,
"The desire of the lazy one puts him to death, for his hands refuse
to work." Spiritual laziness is especially dangerous. That's when we
don't care enough to read our Bible or go to church or pray to our
heavenly Father.

The Bible has an interesting command to those who are lazy:
"Go to the ant, you lazy one. Observe its ways and be wise, which,
having no chief, officer, or ruler, prepares its food in the summer and
gathers its provision in the harvest" (Proverbs 6:6–8). In its own way,
the ant understands that work is an investment. It diligently gathers
food while it's available and stores it away. The ant understands that
a time of plenty is the perfect time to prepare for a time of need. So

it puts in the work to prepare for winter when provisions are scarce and life is harder.

That's the reality God wants us to understand. Spiritual work is an investment. Making the effort to study Scripture, go to church, and spend time daily in prayer has immediate benefits, of course. But it also has long-term benefits. Being grounded in Scripture can help us resist Satan's temptations, as it did for Jesus during His temptation in the wilderness (Matthew 4:1–11). Surrounding ourselves with a network of fellow believers can inspire us to live out our faith in bold and impactful ways. That's why Hebrews 10:24–25 says, "Let's consider how to encourage one another in love and good deeds, not abandoning our own meeting together, as is the habit of some people, but encouraging one another; and all the more as you see the day drawing near." Staying in constant communication with our heavenly Father can help us recognize His will for our lives.

To enjoy these spiritual benefits, we must resist the pull of laziness and stay disciplined in every area of our spiritual life. We must stay constantly aware that the work we do now to understand Scripture, build relationships with fellow believers, and maintain an open line of communication with God will pay dividends for the rest of our life.

DIG DEEP

Laziness can seem like harmless self-indulgence, but that's what makes it so dangerous in our walk with Christ. We confuse doing our own thing with doing nothing. Ask yourself the following questions and answer them truthfully:

1. How have you been lazy in your spiritual life?
2. What habits can you develop to help you prevent laziness from getting a foothold?

Dead to Sin

Because you are sons, God has sent the Spirit of His Son into our hearts, crying, "Abba! Father!" Therefore you are no longer a slave, but a son; and if a son, then an heir through God.
—GALATIANS 4:6–7

BECOMING DEAD TO SIN MAY SEEM LIKE AN UNREACHABLE goal, especially if we continue to lose battles against temptation. But the Bible assures us that sin has no power over us—not because of anything we've done but because of what Christ did on the cross. In John 14:16–28 Jesus promised His disciples that when He returned to heaven, the Holy Spirit would come and dwell inside every reborn believer.

The Holy Spirit connects us with Jesus. Paul said, "But the one who joins himself to the Lord is one spirit with Him" (1 Corinthians 6:17). Through the Holy Spirit we have access to Christ's victory and power over sin. This victory has profound implications for our old sinful nature. Romans 6:6 says, "Our old self was crucified with Him, in order that our body of sin might be done away with, so that we would no longer be slaves to sin." Jesus made that old sinful nature ineffective. We're no longer enslaved to it. When we act in faith and walk in the Spirit, sin is powerless against us.

Romans 6:8–11 says, "Now if we have died with Christ, we believe that we shall also live with Him, knowing that Christ, having been raised from the dead, is never to die again; death no longer is master over Him. For the death that He died, He died to sin once for all time; but the life that He lives, He lives to God. So you too, consider yourselves to be dead to sin, but alive to God in Christ Jesus." *Dead to sin, but alive to God in Christ Jesus*—that's what we strive to be.

We must recognize that the person we used to be died with Christ. That's what water baptism represents. Our submersion represents our dying and being buried with Christ. Our emerging from the water represents being raised to a new life—a life lived in faith and in the Spirit. Because of Christ's victory, we have no reason to fear temptation. We can have confidence in the Holy Spirit's work in us. Sin is no longer inevitable. God equips us with everything we need to stay dead to sin and alive to Him. We just have to access it, because it is impossible to overcome sin by ourselves. We do this by handing over the reins of our life to the Holy Spirit and allowing Him to guide us. We do it by turning to God immediately when we are tempted, instead of giving sin a second thought. We do it by embracing our new life in Christ and choosing to live in the Spirit at all times.

DIG DEEP

The only power your old nature has over you is the power you give it. If you walk in the Spirit, you are dead to sin. Ask yourself the following questions and answer them truthfully:

1. How do you interact with the Holy Spirit when you are faced with temptation?
2. In what areas of your life have you experienced victory over temptation? In what areas are you still struggling?

Jesus and the Fig Tree

As they were passing by in the morning, they
saw the fig tree withered from the roots up.
—MARK 11:20

THE STORY OF JESUS AND THE FIG TREE REALLY HAS nothing to do with hunger or figs and everything to do with spiritual fruit. This story, about the only destructive miracle Jesus ever performed, gives us important insight into our Lord's priorities.

As Jesus was traveling from Bethany to the temple in Jerusalem, He got hungry. Mark 11:13–14 says, "Seeing from a distance a fig tree in leaf, He went to see if perhaps He would find anything on it; and when He came to it, He found nothing but leaves, for it was not the season for figs. And He said to it, 'May no one ever eat fruit from you again!' And His disciples were listening."

To understand the story, you have to know that the fruit of fig trees grows before the leaves do. So if you saw a leafy fig tree, as Jesus did, you would expect to find fruit. The tree gave the impression that it was bearing fruit when it really wasn't. That prompted Jesus to curse the tree so that it would never bear fruit again.

Jesus was making a spiritual point. Immediately after His encounter with the tree, He went to the temple in Jerusalem, the center of Jewish worship. The people there—especially those in charge—put on a great show of being religious. Their outside appearance—their spiritual "leaves"—gave the impression that they were bearing spiritual fruit. But Jesus could see their hearts. And He could see that they were spiritually barren.

Israel had been God's people for thousands of years. They should have known how to produce spiritual fruit, especially the leaders. Yet most of them still had not produced spiritual fruit; they were spiritually dead and had no real relationship with God. And God's patience had worn out. When Jesus and His disciples returned to Bethany, they saw that the fig tree had already withered and died. The Jewish system of worship would face a similar fate. Forty years after these events, the temple in Jerusalem was destroyed.

Jesus' warning wasn't just to the Jewish people, however. Anyone who claims to follow Christ but doesn't bear fruit will ultimately answer to God. Those who do not bear fruit need to examine themselves to see if they truly are in the faith. In John 15:5–6, Jesus said, "I am the vine, you are the branches; the one who remains in Me and I in him, he bears much fruit, for apart from Me you can do nothing. If anyone does not remain in Me, he is thrown away like a branch and dries up; and they gather them and throw them into the fire, and they are burned."

DIG DEEP

In Colossians 1:10, Paul instructed reborn believers to "walk in a manner worthy of the Lord, to please Him in all respects, bearing fruit in every good work and increasing in the knowledge of God." Ask yourself the following questions and answer them truthfully:

1. Why is it so damaging to look as though you're bearing spiritual fruit without actually bearing spiritual fruit?
2. What does spiritual fruit look like in your life and can other people see it clearly?

True Revival

Will You not revive us again, so that
Your people may rejoice in You?
—PSALM 85:6

"REVIVE" MEANS TO BREATHE NEW LIFE INTO SOME-
thing. The Hebrew word *ruach* refers to God's "breath" or "Spirit."
We need God's *ruach* for spiritual revival, just like a drowning person
needs breath to be revived.

A whole nation can lose focus on God over time. In the Old
Testament we see how the Israelites worshiped God, but the people
gradually turned away from God until there was only a remnant left.
God sent His prophets to preach with the power of the Holy Spirit,
and thousands turned back to Him. In the New Testament God used
the apostles to bring revival to His people.

One of the best examples of revival is found in Acts 2. Jesus had
returned to heaven and His disciples were in Jerusalem. "When the
day of Pentecost had come, they were all together in one place. And
suddenly a noise like a violent rushing wind came from heaven, and
it filled the whole house where they were sitting" (verses 1–2).

Peter, filled with the power of the Holy Spirit, preached to the
people. "'Repent, and each of you be baptized in the name of Jesus
Christ for the forgiveness of your sins; and you will receive the gift of
the Holy Spirit.' . . . So then, those who had received his word were
baptized; and that day there were added about three thousand souls"
(verses 38, 41).

True revival is a work of God at a specific time and place over many people, where they repent and accept Him as Lord and Savior. But you can also ask Him for it on a personal level, to reveal Himself to you more and to fill you with the power of the Holy Spirit for ministry. First, you need to fervently pray until God pours out His Spirit with power on you. This will also require you to fully surrender every aspect of your life to Him. He equips you with everything you need to accomplish His purpose for your life. The Holy Spirit also makes you aware of your need for forgiveness. He pulls you out of your comfort zone by shifting your focus away from all the wrong things and back onto Him alone. He reveals to you His presence, His holiness, righteousness, and love. When this happens, all you can do is try to stop the tears from rolling down your cheeks while you repent and ask Him to lead you forward.

If you humbly open your heart to God, He will breathe new life into your prayers, your Bible study, your witness, and every other area of your Christian faith. That's how revival begins. And that's how lives are changed. We need an attitude of brokenness, desperation, and patience to pray for revival. Sisters Peggy and Christine Smith prayed for years until revival broke out in the Hebrides Island. The Moravian revival as well as the revivals under Whitefield, the Wesleys, Moody, and others were all preceded by much prayer.

DIG DEEP

Before the disciples experienced the revival at Pentecost, they prayed fervently for God to ignite their ministry. Prayer is the fuse that lights revival. Ask yourself the following questions and answer them truthfully:

1. Are you prepared to pray for revival in your church or community—even if it takes years?
2. How can you prepare yourself for true revival?

A Husband's Role in Marriage

*Husbands, love your wives, just as Christ also loved
the church and gave Himself up for her.*
—Ephesians 5:25

GOD CREATED MARRIAGE. HE UNDERSTANDS THE RELA-
tional math that allows two to become one without subtracting
anything. He designed us so that we can connect in an extraordinary
way with someone else—and experience amazing love, joy, and fulfillment from that connection. So when God talks about marriage in
His Word, we should pay attention.

Unfortunately, there are a lot of people who aren't paying attention. Studies show that over the past forty years, the divorce rate
has more than doubled globally. Combating this trend begins with
understanding the unique roles God created for husbands and wives
within marriage. Let's look at what God's Word says about the role
of a husband. Ephesians 5:25, 28–30 says, "Husbands, love your wives,
just as Christ also loved the church and gave Himself up for her. . . .
So husbands also ought to love their own wives as their own bodies.
He who loves his own wife loves himself; for no one ever hated his
own flesh, but nourishes and cherishes it, just as Christ also does the
church, because we are parts of His body."

The love Paul is talking about is a commitment to actively
love your spouse even when you're not feeling the romance (eros
love). Paul is talking about *agape* love, the sacrificial love that Christ
has for the church. This love is forgiving; it compels us to work to
restore our relationship after we've been wronged. Sacrificial love

is encouraging; it's quick to overlook mistakes and annoyances. It's humbling; it inspires us to make our own needs and wants secondary.

God demands that we as men treat our wives in an understanding way, realizing that they are unique and different. We need to treat them gently, with love and patience, in the same way God takes care of us. It is so important to Him that if we do not obey Him in this, our prayers will be hindered (1 Peter 3:7).

In Matthew 19:4–6, Jesus emphasized the sacred nature of the marriage relationship. Responding to a question about divorce, He said, "Have you not read that He who created them from the beginning made them male and female, and said, 'For this reason a man shall leave his father and mother and be joined to his wife, and the two shall become one flesh'? So they are no longer two, but one flesh. Therefore, what God has joined together, no person is to separate." Marriage isn't just a promise between a husband and wife; it's also a promise to God—a promise to remain with your spouse for the rest of your life. It's a promise that takes quite a bit of work to fulfill. Falling in love is easy; staying in love is a challenge for most people. The key to a successful marriage lies in having agape love at all times through the Spirit. If you always put God first, you will have an amazing marriage.

DIG DEEP

In Ephesians 5:23, Paul said, "For the husband is the head of the wife, as Christ also is the head of the church." If a husband takes this responsibility seriously and leads in a Christlike way, his wife and children will gladly follow him. Ask yourself the following questions and answer them truthfully:

1. Do you lead your wife in a loving and gentle manner like Christ leads the church?
2. What does a husband's sacrificial love look like in a healthy marriage?

A Wife's Role in Marriage

Wives, subject yourselves to your own husbands, as to the Lord.
—EPHESIANS 5:22

PROVERBS 31:10 TELLS US THAT "AN EXCELLENT WIFE . . . is far above jewels." The Bible emphasizes the value of a wife because marriage is a coming together of two equals, each with essential responsibilities to fulfill. That truth must not be overlooked, especially when one essential responsibility of a wife is to "subject" herself, or submit, to her husband's leadership (Ephesians 5:22).

In the wrong context, the concept of submission might suggest that the wife is less important than or inferior to the husband. But that's not the case in a God-honoring marriage. Paul was talking about voluntary submission. A husband cannot demand it, nor should he have to. In God's plan for marriage, a husband's sacrificial love for his wife will inspire her submission. She can submit for the sake of the marriage, safe in the knowledge that her husband will not take advantage of his authority. Paul also made it clear that when a wife voluntarily submits to her husband, she also submits to Christ.

The husband's responsibility is to lead his wife as Christ leads the church. Jesus came to earth to serve, and He died for us. He showed us how to live for God. In the same way, husbands need to lead by example and live in obedience to God and His Word, because if we do, our wives will do the same.

There is much more to the role of a wife than submission. She is also instrumental in establishing a culture of respect in the home. In Ephesians 5:33, Paul said, "The wife must see to it that she respects her husband." How does she do that? We find the answer in Proverbs 31: "She opens her mouth in wisdom, and the teaching of kindness is on her tongue" (verse 26). She understands how to build up her husband, how to advise him wisely, and how to set a tone of kindness and caring for her entire household.

A wife provides strength and support for her husband. It's been said that the husband is the head and the wife is the neck, the essential support that allows the head to maneuver. A husband cannot fulfill his God-given responsibilities without the strength and support of his wife. That support involves encouraging him when he obeys God's will and lovingly confronting him when he doesn't.

In God's plan for marriage, husbands and wives are encouraged to enter into the union with a spirit of selflessness, service, accountability, and respect for each other. When those qualities are present, the marriage is, as the writer of Ecclesiastes said, "a cord of three strands"—the husband, the wife, and God Himself—"not quickly torn apart" (4:12).

DIG DEEP

A God-honoring marriage is made up of two equally strong people who are willing to sacrifice their own needs and wants for the sake of their relationship. Ask yourself the following questions and answer them truthfully:

1. Do you lead your wife in such a way that it allows her to fulfill her God-given responsibilities in marriage?
2. What does a wife's strength and support look like in a healthy marital relationship?

What About Baptism?

*"Go therefore and make disciples of all the
nations, baptizing them in the name of the
Father and the Son and the Holy Spirit."*
—MATTHEW 28:19

MATTHEW 3 RECORDS A RARE OCCURRENCE IN SCRIPTURE.
All three Persons of the Trinity—God the Father, God the Son, and
God the Holy Spirit—are mentioned as witnesses to a single event:
the baptism of Jesus. Thirty years after Jesus came to earth in human
form, He began His public ministry by requesting that John the
Baptist baptize Him. After Jesus emerged from the Jordan River,
the Holy Spirit descended from heaven like a dove. And God the
Father said: "This is My beloved Son, with whom I am well-pleased"
(verse 17).

The presence of all three members of the Trinity speaks to the
importance of baptism, but it doesn't tell us *why* it's important. For
that, we need to turn to other Scripture passages.

Let's start with the one above: Matthew 28:19. The reference
to the Holy Spirit is important because the day you became a real
reborn Christian, you were baptized with the Holy Spirit. That
means God sent His Spirit to live inside you and to work a profound
change within you.

When you were baptized with the Holy Spirit, you became part
of the body of Christ. You became spiritually connected to everyone
else who's been baptized with the Holy Spirit. Paul explained it this
way: "For even as the body is one and yet has many parts, and all

the parts of the body, though they are many, are one body, so also is Christ. For by one Spirit we were all baptized into one body, whether Jews or Greeks, whether slaves or free, and we were all made to drink of one Spirit" (1 Corinthians 12:12–13).

Baptism with water is a reenactment of the baptism of the Spirit. When you accept and believe that Jesus Christ died for your sins, you die with Christ. Your old nature, the person you used to be, is replaced by a new nature. That's what it means to be born again. Paul said, "Therefore we have been buried with Him through baptism into death, so that just as Christ was raised from the dead through the glory of the Father, so we too may walk in newness of life" (Romans 6:4).

Being submerged in water represents the death and burial of your old self. Emerging from the water represents spiritual rebirth. When you are baptized, you openly say to the world that you are a real reborn Christian. You've turned away from your old, sinful lifestyle and embraced a new, Christlike lifestyle. Baptism is a way of showing others what God has done for you—and what He can do for them.

─────── DIG DEEP ───────

Referring to Peter's preaching of salvation at Pentecost, Acts 2:41 says, "Those who had received his word were baptized." Water baptism is an act of obedience, a way of showing the world what God has done inside you with the baptism of the Holy Spirit. Ask yourself the following questions and answer them truthfully:

1. What does baptism mean to you?
2. What "died" when you went into the water?
3. What is different about the new life you embraced when you came up out of the water?

A Prayer to Start the Day

In the early morning, while it was still dark,
Jesus got up, left the house, and went away to a
secluded place, and prayed there for a time.
—MARK 1:35

LAMENTATIONS 3:22–23 SAYS, "THE LORD'S ACTS OF mercy indeed do not end, for His compassions do not fail. They are new every morning; great is Your faithfulness." Shouldn't there be a prayer to celebrate the fact that God offers fresh blessings every day? Shouldn't we respond to His mercies with a prayer to greet each new day?

Jesus certainly thought so. The passage from Mark quoted above suggests that He made a habit of rising early so that He could spend time in prayer. That's how the Lord prepared for the day ahead. If you'd like to follow His example, here's a sample prayer you can use to start your day.

———

Father in heaven,

Thank You for the privilege of calling You *Father*. I know that I have done nothing to deserve that honor. In Your mercy, You declared me to be Your child when I repented, believed, and accepted that Jesus died in my place for my sins.

There is no greater name than Yours. You are Yahweh, God of all that lives and breathes. Time has no power over You, for You live in it and outside of it. You are the same yesterday, today, and tomorrow. Space has no power over You. You are everywhere; Your eye is on everything.

You created me, and I am just a small piece of Your big puzzle. But I am honored and always willing to abide in You and to do Your will.

I rely on You to give me what I need every day—food for my body and food for my soul that will help me grow spiritually, stronger in You. You are the potter, and I am the clay. You made me. You gave me everything I have, including my talents and abilities. Guide me today so that I might use them to accomplish Your will and bring glory to You.

Work through Your Holy Spirit to direct my path so that I make decisions that honor You. Search my heart, Lord, and take out everything that is not good in Your eyes.

Forgive me for my sins and help me remember Your forgiveness when the time comes for me to forgive others. Help me see other people as You see them. Lord, I am ready to take on the challenges of this day because this is a day that You have made. Lead me forward with the power of Your Spirit so that I will be a light to the world.

In Jesus' name, amen.

DIG DEEP

Paul said, "Do not be anxious about anything, but in everything by prayer and pleading with thanksgiving let your requests be made known to God. And the peace of God, which surpasses all comprehension, will guard your hearts and minds in Christ Jesus" (Philippians 4:6–7). Ask yourself the following questions and answer them truthfully:

1. How many times in the last week have you started your day in prayer?
2. What's the biggest obstacle you face in doing so?
3. How does morning prayer set the tone for your day?

More Than Love

Know therefore that the LORD your God, He is God,
the faithful God, who keeps His covenant and His
faithfulness to a thousand generations for those
who love Him and keep His commandments.
—DEUTERONOMY 7:9

IS THERE ONE WORD THAT PERFECTLY DESCRIBES YOU?
Probably not. Trying to reduce you to a single word makes you less
than you actually are. Anyone who tried to do it would show that
they don't know you very well.

Many people make this mistake with God. They try to summa-
rize His character by using just one passage from the Bible, such as
"God is love" (1 John 4:8). Then they go one step further by arguing
that if you love someone, you want them to be happy. So, they say,
God is okay with whatever makes us happy, even if it goes against
other parts of the Bible.

The problem is, when we focus only on God's love, we miss
other equally important aspects of His nature, including His holiness and justice. In John 3:16 God's love is tied directly to His desire
to save us from sin: "For God so loved the world, that He gave His
only Son, so that everyone who believes in Him shall not perish, but
have eternal life."

David knew God as well as anyone ever has. Look at his words
in Psalm 139:23–24: "Search me, God, and know my heart; put me to
the test and know my anxious thoughts; and see if there is any hurt-
ful way in me, and lead me in the everlasting way." David understood

that sin interfered with his relationship with God, so he wanted his heavenly Father to make him aware of any disobedience in his heart.

You'll notice that everyone who had a personal relationship with God in Scripture approached Him with reverence. In Genesis 3:10 Adam and Eve hid from God after they disobeyed Him. In Exodus 3:6 Moses hid his face from God. In 2 Samuel 6:9, when David saw God's power at work, he was afraid. These people understood God's holiness and justice—not just His love—and they were rightly intimidated by them.

God is much more than just love. He reveals His many other attributes through His Word. Romans 1:19–20 says, "Because that which is known about God is evident within them; for God made it evident to them. For since the creation of the world His invisible attributes, His eternal power and divine nature, have been clearly perceived, being understood by what has been made, so that they are without excuse." Likewise, we cannot just say "God is love" and use that as an excuse to sin, because by doing so we ignore that He is also holy and righteous. Our main goal of our walk with God is to be like Jesus Christ. We need to live holy lives because God is holy.

DIG DEEP

Understanding God's love is a great starting point in getting to know Him. But if that's where you stop, you don't have the opportunity to more fully know Him. Ask yourself the following questions and answer them truthfully:

1. Why is it dangerous to believe that God's love means all He wants is for you to be happy?
2. Why is obedience more important to God than your happiness?

What It Means to Tithe

Honor the LORD from your wealth, and
from the first of all your produce.
—PROVERBS 3:9

WHY DOES GOD NEED OUR MONEY? THAT'S THE QUESTION
a lot of believers struggle with. We hear calls to tithe what God has given us and wonder why He needs our meager contributions to fund His work. After all, He is God. He could fill the bank accounts of every ministry on earth if He wanted to.

Tithing isn't a fundraising strategy; it's a spiritual discipline. Practicing it gives reborn believers a chance to be a part of God's ministry on earth. It gives us a deeper appreciation for God's blessings in our lives and emphasizes our responsibility to people in need. It also teaches us to be wise stewards of our money, our talents and abilities, and our time.

The topic of tithing is about much more than finances. It's about understanding that everything we have comes from God—and then living in a way that reflects this understanding. God sets the example for us. James 1:5 says, "If any of you lacks wisdom, let him ask of God, who gives to all generously and without reproach, and it will be given to him."

One of the most frequent questions reborn believers ask about tithing is how much to give. Should we give 10 percent of our income? Fifteen percent? Twenty percent? Some people point out that the word "tithe" means "one-tenth." But there's a biblical truth here that cannot be overlooked. God gives generously to all, and He appreciates when we do the same. Look at Paul's words in 2 Corinthians 9:6–7: "Now I say this: the one who sows sparingly will also reap sparingly, and the one who sows generously will also reap generously. Each one must do just as he has decided in his heart, not reluctantly or under compulsion, for God loves a cheerful giver."

Ultimately, tithing is a discipline that begins in the heart. If we delight in sharing with others what God has blessed us with, the percentages will take care of themselves. If we're attuned to God's blessings in our lives and to the needs of the people around us, the Holy Spirit will guide us in our giving, which is also a way of multiplying our blessings. Acts 20:35 says, "In everything I showed you that by working hard in this way you must help the weak and remember the words of the Lord Jesus, that He Himself said, 'It is more blessed to give than to receive.'" That's what's amazing about God's design. The purpose of tithing isn't to gain personally. It isn't a wealth-building strategy. God blesses us through the act of giving—not in material ways but in spiritual ways. Tithing helps us to overcome the sin of greed, to let go of our material possessions, and it lets us share in His plan. It gives us a sense of purpose. And it grows our faith in amazing ways.

DIG DEEP

God entrusts His blessings to you not just for your own sake but also for the sake of others. Tithing gives you opportunities to make a difference in others' lives. Ask yourself the following questions and answer them truthfully:

1. Do you think God blesses certain people with money, talents, or gifts to enjoy only for themselves or to use for His glory?
2. What are things you consider when deciding how much to tithe?
3. Are you a cheerful giver or do you struggle to let go of what God gave you in the first place?

Christians and Politics

"Then pay to Caesar the things that are Caesar's;
and to God the things that are God's."
—MATTHEW 22:21

IN THE BODY OF CHRIST, DISCUSSING POLITICS CAN KILL
fellowship instantly if someone says the wrong thing. The irony is
that many reborn believers who break fellowship over political differences believe they're doing what God wants them to do. But is the
Holy Spirit leading them to leave the fellowship, or are they acting
out of their flesh while using their faith to rationalize their decision?

God's kingdom is much bigger and more important than this
world and its politics. The kingdom of God "is not of this world"
(John 18:36), but it influences this world. We are in a fight between
light and dark. Jesus came to live with us physically in human form
so that we might gain spiritual life! There are spiritual forces at work
behind what we can see with our physical eyes. Many believers mistakenly fight the physical instead of combating the spiritual forces.
We need to remember that "our struggle is not against flesh and
blood, but against the rulers, against the powers, against the world
forces of this darkness, against the spiritual forces of wickedness in
the heavenly places" (Ephesians 6:12).

The devil will try to distract us to focus on the wrong things, but
our top priority is furthering God's kingdom and adding people to
it. We need to share the gospel and stand up for what is right in this
temporary world. Jesus said, "Seek first His kingdom and His righteousness, and all these things will be provided to you" (Matthew 6:33).

Earthly politics often seem to defy God's purposes and priorities. Sadly, many politicians treat political power as a license to indulge in corruption and greed. Their promises are almost always suspect. Their "truth" is rarely true. If we want truth, we must go to the Source. Jesus said to His followers, "If you continue in My word, then you are truly My disciples; and you will know the truth, and the truth will set you free" (John 8:31–32). Never look to political leaders for things only Jesus can offer.

Our responsibility to God's kingdom and truth does not place us above human government. As reborn believers we don't get to choose which earthly authorities we will recognize as legitimate. Paul said in Romans 13:1–2, "Every person is to be subject to the governing authorities. For there is no authority except from God, and those which exist are established by God. Therefore whoever resists authority has opposed the ordinance of God; and they who have opposed will receive condemnation upon themselves."

In Titus 3:1–2, Paul said, "Remind them to be subject to rulers, to authorities, to be obedient, to be ready for every good deed, to slander no one, not to be contentious, to be gentle, showing every consideration for all people." His point is clear. Though it's tempting to actively promote our political beliefs, as reborn believers we can have more of an impact on our community by obeying God's Word.

DIG DEEP

You can't avoid politics altogether. But you can keep it in proper perspective, especially in relation to God's kingdom. Ask yourself the following questions and answer them truthfully:

1. What are the primary causes of political division among your family, friends, and acquaintances?
2. How can you find fellowship with reborn believers who disagree with you politically?

A Godly Response to Scandal

Be on guard for yourselves and for all the flock, among which the Holy Spirit has made you overseers, to shepherd the church of God which He purchased with His own blood.
—ACTS 20:28

TOO OFTEN WE SEE HEADLINES PROCLAIMING THAT another Christian leader has been caught up in a scandal. If the leader is someone you respected, you may question the validity of his teaching. You may wonder whether other Christians are who they claim to be. You may start to feel cynical about the Christian faith. A scandal may cause a season of spiritual darkness, but if you keep a few truths in mind, you can weather the storm.

First, *recognize that the few do not represent the many.* There are countless Christian leaders who work faithfully and humbly in their communities to further God's kingdom without a hint of controversy. They set an example for other believers in their "speech, conduct, love, faith and purity" (1 Timothy 4:12). The scandalous actions of certain well-known Christian leaders do nothing to taint the work of these faithful leaders.

Second, *put your faith in God and His Word, not in Christian leaders.* Just because a Christian leader you like says something does not make it true. Make sure that every message aligns with the truth of Scripture. Paul said, "Examine everything; hold firmly to that which is good" (1 Thessalonians 5:21).

Third, *don't draw conclusions based on incomplete facts.* Don't pass rumors as truth. Consider James's warning: "Do not speak against one another, brothers and sisters. The one who speaks against a brother or sister, or judges his brother or sister, speaks against the law and judges the law; but if you judge the law, you are not a doer of the law but a judge of it" (James 4:11).

Fourth, *pray*. Paul said, "I urge that requests, prayers, intercession, and thanksgiving be made in behalf of all people, for kings and all who are in authority, so that we may lead a tranquil and quiet life in all godliness and dignity" (1 Timothy 2:1–2). Pray for the people involved in the scandal. Pray for their families. Pray for the church. Pray for wisdom and discernment. Ask God to bring something good from something bad.

Fifth, *judge righteously*. John 7:24 says, "Do not judge by the outward appearance, but judge with righteous judgment." Be careful when you suspect a wolf is disguised as a sheep. You can play right into the devil's hand by destroying many lives if you judge wrongly. And be careful how you react. Considering how quickly people gossip and judge Christian leaders today, many of them would probably have called David a false prophet after his sins regarding Bathsheba. David, however, truly loved God and repented. There are spiritual leaders who truly love God, but they may fall into sin—like David did—for a short time. A spiritual leader is a human with a fleshly nature just like you; we are all capable of any sin. But true reborn Christians will not continue to live in sin. You will know them by their fruit!

———————— DIG DEEP ————————

We must hold our Christian leaders to the standards set in God's Word. But we must also be ready to forgive as we have been forgiven. Ask yourself the following questions and answer them truthfully:

1. Why is cynicism an especially dangerous response to a Christian who is involved in a scandal?
2. What would you say to someone who pointed to scandals involving Christians as a reason for not being a reborn believer?

How Often Should You Repent?

"Forgive us our debts, as we also have forgiven our debtors.
And do not lead us into temptation, but deliver us from evil."
—MATTHEW 6:12–13

JESUS SET THE BAR FOR HOLY LIVING EXTREMELY HIGH.
In the Sermon on the Mount, He explained that sinful behavior starts with our thoughts. He said, "You have heard that it was said, 'You shall not commit adultery'; but I say to you that everyone who looks at a woman with lust for her has already committed adultery with her in his heart" (Matthew 5:27–28).

Every time your brain generates a thought, you have a chance to sin. Every time your eye lingers over someone, you have a chance to sin. Every time you react to someone who annoys you, you have a chance to sin.

That's a problem because sin interferes with your relationship with God. It doesn't change your status as His child. That's important to understand. If you've accepted Christ as your Savior, you've been declared righteous. Paul said, "But now apart from the Law the righteousness of God has been revealed, being witnessed by the Law and the Prophets, but it is the righteousness of God through faith in Jesus Christ for all those who believe; for there is no distinction; for all have sinned and fall short of the glory of God, being justified as a gift by His grace through the redemption which is in Christ Jesus" (Romans 3:21–24).

Being declared righteous isn't the same as being perfect. You still have a sinful nature inside you. Sometimes that nature will get the better of you. Sometimes you'll lose the battle against temptation.

That doesn't mean you have to become spiritually reborn again; it only happens once. Justification happens once. God put His Spirit in you. That's why Paul said, "Do not grieve the Holy Spirit of God, by whom you were sealed for the day of redemption" (Ephesians 4:30). The Holy Spirit is sealed inside you. Sin doesn't take away your salvation.

Sin does, however, create a wall between you and God, and keep you from enjoying everything God has to offer. And it keeps you from living the life He intends for you. That's why the Holy Spirit makes His grieving known. He acts stronger than your conscience. He lets you know when something's not right inside you—when there's a temporary blockage in your relationship with God. He makes you feel bad about what you've done—not to ruin your self-esteem but to compel you to take care of the problem. When the Holy Spirit convicts you of a sin, you should ask God's forgiveness immediately—never put it aside until later.

The Holy Spirit works in you until you say, "Father, I messed up. Please forgive me for what I've done. Restore Your relationship with me." Never let sin or any obstacle influence you to walk outside the will of God and not within it. The writer of Hebrews said, "Let's rid ourselves of every obstacle and the sin which so easily entangles us, and let's run with endurance the race that is set before us" (Hebrews 12:1).

DIG DEEP

The Holy Spirit will let you know when you need to repent and ask for forgiveness. If you follow His lead, you'll maintain a healthy, thriving relationship with the Lord. Ask yourself the following questions and answer them truthfully:

1. How does the Holy Spirit convict you of sin?
2. When and how do you react to it?

Does Sin Bother You Like It Should?

Fight the good fight, keeping faith and a good conscience, which some have rejected and suffered shipwreck in regard to their faith.
—1 TIMOTHY 1:18–19

WHEN WE GIVE OUR LIVES TO CHRIST, HE TRANSFORMS everything about us, including our sinful lifestyles. Paul explained it this way: "For you were once darkness, but now you are light in the Lord; walk as children of light (for the fruit of the light consists in all goodness, righteousness, and truth), as you try to learn what is pleasing to the Lord" (Ephesians 5:8–10). Before we were reborn Christians, we preferred to walk in darkness because it was all we knew. Darkness blinded our minds so we could not see or understand the light (2 Corinthians 4:4).

God revealed His light to us, and we know that darkness cannot exist where the Lord is. If we commit to follow Him, we walk in His light. That doesn't make us perfect; we must battle our old sinful nature every day. But the light exposes our sin. It shows us where we fall short of God's glory and His will for our lives. The light gives us the opportunity to repent of and ask forgiveness for the sin it exposes.

Some people, however, are unbothered by what the Lord's light reveals. They reason that because they've been saved by grace, and not by works, they're free to sin. If they didn't do anything to earn their salvation, they can't do anything to lose it. With their conscience dulled, they ignore the prompting of the Holy Spirit.

Frequent repentance and forgiveness are essential to our spiritual growth and maturity. We need to feel deeply the pangs of regret and guilt that prompt us to seek forgiveness. If we do not feel the pangs of regret, we need to examine ourselves to see whether we truly are in the faith. If we really have been transformed by God and received the Holy Spirit, He will convict us of sin in such a powerful way that we cannot ignore it. This is one of the reasons why He came to be with us. Jesus said, "And He, when He comes, will convict the world regarding sin, and righteousness, and judgment" (John 16:8).

You need to take sin seriously to live a holy life. It starts with understanding God's holiness. You do this by drawing close to God. James 4:8 says, "Come close to God and He will come close to you." Spend time in His Word. Let Him work in your heart to repair your conscience. Sin, in its essence, is when you don't obey God. The New Testament says that you are under the law of the Spirit. This means that you will sin every time you do not listen to the Holy Spirit. So let the Holy Spirit guide you in everything you do. Listen and obey.

DIG DEEP

Recognizing the Holy Spirit's work within you is essential to your spiritual health. We cannot live through the Spirit if we do not understand how He works in us and through us. Ask yourself the following questions and answer them truthfully:

1. What does the conviction of the Holy Spirit look like in your life?
2. In what circumstances might you be tempted to ignore the Holy Spirit's guidance?
3. How does keeping your conscience clean help you draw closer to God?

Bible Passages That Changed My Life

For the word of God is living and active, and sharper
than any two-edged sword, even penetrating as far as the
division of soul and spirit, of both joints and marrow, and
able to judge the thoughts and intentions of the heart.
—HEBREWS 4:12

MANY BIBLE PASSAGES HAVE COMPLETELY TRANS-
formed who I am, how I look at the world, and how I live my life.
Scripture shows us the distance between who we are and who God
intends us to be—and then shows us how to close that distance. Paul
explained it this way: "All Scripture is inspired by God and beneficial
for teaching, for rebuke, for correction, for training in righteousness;
so that the man or woman of God may be fully capable, equipped for
every good work" (2 Timothy 3:16–17).

Here are three passages that have profoundly impacted me and
equipped me for God's good work. The first is Matthew 6:33: "But
seek first His kingdom and His righteousness, and all these things
will be provided to you." Jesus explained that reborn believers don't
need to worry about the necessities of life because God knows what
we need. I have discovered that when I make God my top priority,
worries fall away and my needs get taken care of.

The second is Matthew 7:21–23: "Not everyone who says to Me,
'Lord, Lord,' will enter the kingdom of heaven, but the one who
does the will of My Father who is in heaven will enter. Many will
say to Me on that day, 'Lord, Lord, did we not prophesy in Your

name, and in Your name cast out demons, and in Your name per-form many miracles?' And then I will declare to them, 'I never knew you; leave Me, you who practice lawlessness.'" These verses forced me to take a look in the mirror and to take my relationship with God seriously, making sure I live according to God's Word. The idea that some people believe they have a relationship with Christ when they actually don't—it shocked me to my core. I decided to serve Christ in complete devotion, because He calls us to radical discipleship! This is the life we need to live to ensure we don't hear God speak the awful words of Matthew 7:23 on judgment day.

The third is Romans 8:28: "And we know that God causes all things to work together for good to those who love God, to those who are called according to His purpose." God doesn't promise us a trouble-free life. He promises to use all the things that happen—the ups and downs—together for good. This truth helped me realize that the downs we experience are not negative at all when we look at them through the Spirit! All of it is just a life with Christ where He uses people and situations to mold us. Once He has started a work in us He will complete it. He is the potter and we are the clay.

These passages made a huge difference in my life, and I hope they will in yours too.

DIG DEEP

One of the amazing things about God's Word is that certain passages can reveal new meaning or a new application just when you need them to. A Bible verse that barely registers with you today might make a profound impact on your life tomorrow. Ask yourself the following questions and answer them truthfully:

1. How do you make Bible study a top priority in your life?
2. What Bible passages have changed your life?

On the Seventh Day

*Jesus said to them, "The Sabbath was made
for man, and not man for the Sabbath."*
—MARK 2:27

FOR MANY REBORN BELIEVERS, THE SABBATH IS A CON-
fusing concept. Is it something God's people should still observe
today? If so, should we observe it on Saturday, as the people of Israel
practiced? Or should we observe it on Sunday, the day Jesus rose
from the dead? And how should we observe it—by resting or by
worshiping?

To understand what the Sabbath means for reborn believers
today, we must go back to its origins in the Old Testament. Exodus
20:8–11 says, "Remember the Sabbath day, to keep it holy. For six
days you shall labor and do all your work, but the seventh day is a
Sabbath of the LORD your God; on it you shall not do any work. . . .
For in six days the LORD made the heavens and the earth, the sea and
all that is in them, and He rested on the seventh day; therefore the
LORD blessed the Sabbath day and made it holy."

This is one of the Ten Commandments. You'll notice, however,
that the command says nothing about going to church or worshiping on the Sabbath. Instead, the Sabbath was a day of rest. Just as
God rested on the seventh day after His work of creation, His people
were to rest on the seventh day of the week after working the other
six days. And that's how God's people marked the day for centuries.
They followed strict rules that forbade everything from building a
fire to leaving their house on the Sabbath.

The coming of Jesus, however, changed that. Hebrews 4 helps us understand that the Sabbath in the Old Testament pointed to the eternal rest that Jesus would make possible. Jesus said, "Do not presume that I came to abolish the Law or the Prophets; I did not come to abolish but to fulfill" (Matthew 5:17). The Sabbath is included in that. We are no longer responsible to obey Sabbath laws of rest because we have eternal rest through Christ.

There are no rules for us to follow when it comes to the first day of the week. The fact that it's become a day of worship is due to tradition, not a biblical mandate. The early church came together on the first day of the week because the resurrection occurred on the first day of the week (Sunday), but nowhere is this a command in Scripture. And Paul left it up to individual believers to decide whether to observe a day of rest: "The one who observes the day, observes it for the Lord, and the one who eats, does so with regard to the Lord, for he gives thanks to God; and the one who does not eat, it is for the Lord that he does not eat, and he gives thanks to God" (Romans 14:6). And as for worship, that should take place *every* day, not just on Saturday or Sunday.

DIG DEEP

If you're a reborn believer, you're not under the Sabbath law. But you need to worship God every day and can still honor God by setting aside specific time for worship. Ask yourself the following questions and answer them truthfully:

1. Why is it counterproductive to think of Sunday as *the* day of worship?
2. What does daily worship look like in your life?

Finding the Right Church

I am writing these things to you, hoping to come to you before long; but in case I am delayed, I write so that you will know how one should act in the household of God, which is the church of the living God, the pillar and support of the truth.
—1 TIMOTHY 3:14–15

HAVE YOU EVER HEARD THE EXPRESSION "THE WHOLE IS greater than the sum of its parts"? Nowhere is the truth of that statement more obvious than in the church. Individually, the people who make up the church bring a unique set of talents, experiences, opinions, prejudices, and struggles.

But when you put those people together in fellowship, something extraordinary happens. They set aside their differences to share spiritual common ground. They lift their voices together in worship to create a sound that's pleasing to God's ear. They become integral parts of one another's lives. They join together to accomplish God's work in this world, like the various parts of a single body. They encourage, challenge, and confront one another. They hold one another accountable. They pick up those who stumble and care for those in need.

The key to the fellowship experience is Christ Himself. In Matthew 18:20, He said, "For where two or three have gathered together in My name, I am there in their midst." So when we spend time in the presence of other believers, we spend time in the presence of the Lord.

The Bible makes it clear that we cannot fully grow or thrive as reborn believers if we're not part of a church. Hebrews 10:24–25 says, "And let's consider how to encourage one another in love and good deeds, not abandoning our own meeting together, as is the habit of some people, but encouraging one another; and all the more as you see the day drawing near."

If you haven't yet found a church home, you'll need to consider two things in your search. The first is *what a church has to offer you.* If you're a new believer, you'll want to find a church that features solid biblical teaching. If you have kids, you'll want to find a congregation with thriving children's and youth ministries.

The second thing to consider is *what you have to offer the church.* Fellowship and worship aren't spectator sports. The church model laid out in God's Word is not one in which a few people work hard to create a memorable Sunday experience for an audience. Everyone in the church has a spiritual gift, given to them by God to benefit the church and participate in its ministry. If you're not using your gift for that purpose, you're not experiencing fellowship as God intends it. A church can do amazing things for you—and you can do amazing things in your church.

DIG DEEP

You can come up with dozens of reasons not to get involved in church. But none of them is as compelling as the words of Hebrews 10:24–25. Ask yourself the following questions and answer them truthfully:

1. Why is it important for you to join with other reborn believers?
2. What happens when you neglect to meet together with other believers for worship and fellowship?
3. What essential gifts and abilities can you put to use in your church?

Learning to Forgive

"And forgive us our debts, as we also
have forgiven our debtors."
—MATTHEW 6:12

IS IT EASIER TO ASK FOR FORGIVENESS FROM SOMEONE
you hurt or to forgive someone who hurt you? The obstacles that
make asking for forgiveness so difficult are pride and shame. We're
either too proud or too embarrassed to admit what we've done.
There are more obstacles to consider.

Holding a grudge allows us to get a measure of revenge and to
feel morally justified in doing so. Forgiving people who wrong us
means giving up that opportunity. True forgiveness also wipes the
slate clean, allowing the people who hurt us to move on with a clear
conscience. That's a difficult thing to ask of a wounded person.

But as reborn believers, we have received the most incredible,
undeserved forgiveness ever offered. Because of Christ's sacrifice,
anyone who truly repents of their sin will be forgiven—forever.
In Hebrews 8:12, God says, "For I will be merciful toward their
wrongdoings, and their sins I will no longer remember." Asking for
forgiveness wipes our slate clean in God's eyes.

When we choose to forgive people who wrong us, we offer a
powerful example of what God does for us. When we refuse, we
send an unmistakable message that we don't appreciate forgiveness.
And that must feel like a slap in the face to the One who forgave us
everything. That's why Jesus said, "For if you forgive other people for
their offenses, your heavenly Father will also forgive you. But if you

do not forgive other people, then your Father will not forgive your offenses" (Matthew 6:14–15).

As the recipients of God's undeserved forgiveness, we don't get to decide who deserves our forgiveness or how often to forgive others. In Matthew 18, Peter probably thought he was being generous when he offered to forgive someone "up to seven times" (verse 21). But Jesus said, "I do not say to you, up to seven times, but up to seventy-seven times" (verse 22). Jesus' point is that we should forgive people unconditionally, just as God forgives us unconditionally. If we want God to forgive us every time we sin, we need to do the same to others.

Offering someone only 99 percent forgiveness is not forgiveness. That is why so many people still hurt and are angry when they remember past experiences. To be 100 percent free, you need to forgive 100 percent.

Forgiving other people doesn't guarantee that your relationship with them will be restored. Paul said, "If possible, so far as it depends on you, be at peace with all people" (Romans 12:18). He also said, "Do not be deceived: 'Bad company corrupts good morals'" (1 Corinthians 15:33). Forgiveness doesn't include allowing people into our lives who don't belong there. Trusting someone and forgiving someone are two different things. You don't have to trust someone who might let you down again, but you have to forgive them.

DIG DEEP

You can't be a Christian without being forgiven and forgiving others. Ask yourself the following questions and answer them truthfully:

1. Why does God ask you to forgive others?
2. Who do you still need to forgive?

Making a Discipline of Bible Study
Getting Started

Be diligent to present yourself approved to God
as a workman who does not need to be ashamed,
accurately handling the word of truth.
—2 TIMOTHY 2:15

THE BIBLE CAN BE INTIMIDATING FOR PEOPLE WHO aren't familiar with it. Its stories involve ancient customs that often make little sense to modern readers. Knowing where to find the wisdom in its pages often requires some work. Proverbs 2:4–5 says, "If you seek [wisdom] as silver and search for her as for hidden treasures; then you will understand the fear of the LORD, and discover the knowledge of God."

Understanding God's Word takes time and effort. But the resulting rewards ensure that our time and effort are the best investments we'll ever make. Paul said, "All Scripture is inspired by God and beneficial for teaching, for rebuke, for correction, for training in righteousness; so that the man or woman of God may be fully capable, equipped for every good work" (2 Timothy 3:16–17).

Here are three ways you can prepare to spend time in Scripture. First, *select the right Bible*. You'll find that there are many different versions and translations. One of my favorites is the New American Standard Bible (Scripture passages in this book come from the NASB). It's easy to understand, and it's one of the best word-for-word translations of the original text. Other translations I enjoy that are both accurate and easy to read are the English Standard Version (ESV), the

Amplified Bible (AMP), the New King James Version (NKJV), and the Christian Standard Bible (CSB).

Second, *choose a setting and time.* Mark 1:35 says, "In the early morning, while it was still dark, Jesus got up, left the house, and went away to a secluded place, and prayed there for a time." Jesus understood that His time with His Father required His complete focus and attention. Find a place where you won't be interrupted or distracted, then set aside a specific time every day to read, contemplate, and pray about God's Word. If you create a daily routine, it will be easier to stick to it when it becomes a habit.

Third, *choose a reading plan.* If you have never read the entire Bible, make that your first goal. This will prevent you from reading only what you want to read and ignoring the parts your flesh may want to avoid. Many believers have been Christians for decades but have never read the entire Bible. I suggest you start in the New Testament with the Gospel of John and read from there through to Revelation. Then start on the Old Testament. After that, choose a specific book to read or a topic to study.

Let the Holy Spirit guide you. Paul said in Philippians 1:6, "For I am confident of this very thing, that He who began a good work among you will perfect it until the day of Christ Jesus." God will help you with your spiritual growth. Trust Him and spend time with Him. Get started today!

DIG DEEP

Meaningful Bible study should be your number-one priority in your daily schedule. Ask yourself the following questions and answer them truthfully:

1. How much time do you think God wants you to spend in His Word each day, and are you doing it?
2. What's the ideal time and place for you to study God's Word?

Making a Discipline of Bible Study
Navigating the Old Testament

Now He said to them, "These are My words which I
spoke to you while I was still with you, that all the
things that are written about Me in the Law of Moses
and the Prophets and the Psalms must be fulfilled."
—LUKE 24:44

THE BIBLE IS UNLIKE ANY OTHER BOOK. SOME PEOPLE
assume it must be read from start to finish. For some, that's an overwhelming thought because the Bible begins with the Old Testament,
an intimidating collection of thirty-nine books, some of which are 50,
66, and even 150 chapters long.

There is not just one "right" way to read the Bible. It isn't a novel
or arranged chronologically, so it doesn't have to be read from start
to finish. In fact, I recommend that people begin with the New
Testament because it's a little easier to understand. The knowledge
gained from reading the New Testament will also help you to better
understand the Old Testament.

The Old Testament isn't as intimidating as it seems. It contains
some of the most famous events ever recorded—including the flood,
the parting of the Red Sea, and David's victory over Goliath. Some of
the most famous people who ever lived—including Abraham, Moses,
and Solomon—are found there too. And so are some of the most
famous words of wisdom and inspiration, including "The LORD is my
shepherd, I will not be in need" (Psalm 23:1) and "There is a time for
every matter under heaven" (Ecclesiastes 3:1).

When you read the Old Testament, you will also discover passages that you have never heard preached in church. I remember how surprised I was when I read specific details about the mighty heroes who fought with David. If you're up for the challenge, be ready to be amazed at what you find in the Old Testament.

Jesus set the example by making the Old Testament Scriptures a priority in His life. He quoted from fourteen different books in the Old Testament, treating all of them as absolute truth. It will also surprise you to see how Jesus Himself is also in the Old Testament.

You can begin your study of the Old Testament in any number of places. The Pentateuch (Genesis through Deuteronomy) shows how everything began, especially God's covenant with His people. The historical books (Joshua through Esther) show how the obedience or disobedience of God's people led to the blessings or curses of the covenant. The poetic books (Job through Song of Solomon) collect the wisdom and observations of people who were given insight into God's nature and human nature. The prophetic books (Isaiah through Malachi) remind God's people of their covenant responsibilities and include prophecies of the coming Savior.

If we ask God to guide our study, He will reveal His truth to us through His Holy Spirit.

DIG DEEP

To fully appreciate who Jesus is and what He accomplished, we need to read the Old Testament. Ask yourself the following questions and answer them truthfully:

1. How much do you really know about the Old Testament, and how much do you think God wants you to know?
2. How would you prefer to incorporate the Old Testament into your Bible study?

Making a Discipline of Bible Study
Exploring the New Testament

*For this reason we also constantly thank God that when
you received the word of God which you heard from us, you
accepted it not as the word of mere men, but as what it really
is, the word of God, which also is at work in you who believe.*
—1 THESSALONIANS 2:13

WITHOUT THE NEW TESTAMENT, WE WOULD HAVE NO
idea how to follow Christ. After all, living as a reborn believer
means constantly asking ourselves, *What would Jesus do?* To answer
that question, though, we must know what Jesus did. We also must
understand the implications of His life and ministry as God and man.
And that knowledge is found exclusively in the New Testament.

The four Gospels that begin the New Testament form the cen-
terpiece of the Bible. The books that come before them—that is, the
entire Old Testament—set the stage for the arrival of the Savior.
Matthew, Mark, Luke, and John show us what happened when He
arrived. Guided by the Holy Spirit, the four authors of the Gospels
shared eyewitness accounts of Jesus' time on earth.

At the end of his biography, John said, "But there are also many
other things which Jesus did, which, if they were written in detail,
I expect that even the world itself would not contain the books that
would be written" (John 21:25). He understood that he was tackling
a huge subject. But in four short books, he and his fellow gospel
writers managed to give us a detailed account of Jesus' ministry,
His miracles, His teachings, His priorities, His interactions with His

followers and foes, and His saving work. Virtually everything we know about Jesus comes from the Gospels. That's why they are the ideal place to begin a Bible study.

The twenty-three books that follow the Gospels—the rest of the New Testament—help us understand how Jesus' coming impacted the world and, more importantly, what it means to us, now and forever. The book of Acts tells how Jesus' followers started the church and spread His message throughout the world.

The letters of Paul, James, Peter, John, and Jude, and the book of Hebrews lay out the theology of Christianity. They explain what we believe and why. They reveal God's plan of salvation. They offer warnings against spiritual pride, worldly living, and false teachings. They encourage us to follow Christ's example and to live our Christian faith in a way that draws others to Him.

The book of Revelation reveals the completion of God's plan, promises the final victory of righteousness over evil, and gives us a glimpse of what eternity will be like for reborn believers.

Together, these books make up *the* essential text for Christ's followers. Studying the New Testament should be at the top of our priority list. Our spiritual growth depends on it.

DIG DEEP

The more time you spend studying the New Testament, praying over it, and applying its truth to your life, the more potent your faith becomes. Ask yourself the following questions and answer them truthfully:

1. Why is it dangerous if you only study the parts of the New Testament that you like and ignore the rest?
2. How does the Holy Spirit help you understand and apply the teachings of the New Testament?

Making a Discipline of Bible Study
Journaling and Prayer

Make me understand the way of Your precepts,
and I will meditate on Your wonders.
—PSALM 119:27

ONE POPULAR METHOD OF INTERACTING WITH GOD'S
Word is to read through the Bible in a year. There are 1,189 chapters
in the Bible, so readers must complete three to four chapters a day.
It's an ambitious goal, the kind that task-oriented people especially
thrive on.

Of course, any plan that involves spending time daily in God's
Word has the potential to change lives, and there are two key spiritual tools that can help you in this area. The first is *prayer*. That's
not surprising. Paul said, "Do not be anxious about anything, but
in everything by prayer and pleading with thanksgiving let your
requests be made known to God" (Philippians 4:6). John said, "This
is the confidence which we have before Him, that, if we ask anything
according to His will, He hears us" (1 John 5:14). The "everything" of
Philippians 4 and the "anything" of 1 John 5 would certainly include
Bible study.

Ideally, your Bible study should begin and end with prayer.
Before you open the pages of Scripture, ask God to bless your study
time. Ask Him to help you focus your thoughts and clear your mind
of distractions. Ask Him to make you receptive to His truth and
attentive to the leading of the Holy Spirit.

After you finish reading, ask Him to engrave His Word on your heart and on the forefront of your mind, so that you can ruminate on it, wrestle with it, and look for ways to apply it in your life. Thank Him for the opportunity to grow closer to Him through His holy Scripture.

The second tool is *journaling*. Taking notes during your study is a great way to help you focus. Instead of reading just to read, you're processing your thoughts and reactions in print. Journaling helps you identify key themes in the passage, consider how it applies to you, and identify how God wants you to respond.

One other key benefit of journaling is that you have a written record of how God has worked in your life. If you start to struggle with doubt or anxiety, you can look back at your journal to see example after example of God's faithfulness in the past. Ideally, your journal will become one of your most treasured possessions, and maybe even your children's when you are with Christ one day. My father's journals are a great blessing to me and my family. We still learn spiritual truths from them today, years after my father passed on to eternal life.

DIG DEEP

If you enlist God's help through prayer and interact with the text through journaling, you will see progress in your Bible study. You will also see amazing changes in your life. Ask yourself the following questions and answer them truthfully:

1. How have you approached reading the Bible in the past? How do you want to approach it now?
2. What do you want to be able to see when you look back over your Bible study journal?

Making a Discipline of Bible Study
Applying God's Truth

"If you know these things, you are blessed if you do them."
—JOHN 13:17

FITNESS EXPERTS SAY THAT IF YOU WORK OUT FIVE DAYS
a week, you'll start to notice visible changes in yourself in about two
weeks. The same principle applies to Bible study, only the changes
are spiritual. And you don't always have to wait two weeks. That's
because studying God's Word isn't just a reading exercise; it's a way
of changing your life. In fact, that's how you know if you're doing it
right: you—and others—start to notice changes in the way you act,
in the decisions you make, and in the way you interact with others.

Jesus said, "Blessed are those who hear the word of God and follow it" (Luke 11:28). Hearing—or studying—God's Word is only the
first step. We must also do what it says. We must live out its truths.

James offered these instructions: "Prove yourselves doers of the
word, and not just hearers who deceive themselves" (James 1:22).
With some passages, the "doing" part is easy to figure out. Let's
say you're studying Jesus' Sermon on the Mount in Matthew 5 and
you come across these words: "Therefore if you are presenting your
offering at the altar, and there you remember that your brother has
something against you, leave your offering there before the altar
and go; first be reconciled to your brother, and then come and present your offering" (verses 23–24). As you think, pray, and journal
about Jesus' words, you realize that reconciliation is so important
to the Lord that He wants you to interrupt your worship to make

amends with an estranged friend. It's only natural that you'd start thinking of people you're estranged from and ways to reconcile with them. That's an obvious application.

With other passages, the application may not be as obvious. So you need to rely more heavily on the Holy Spirit's guidance. Your takeaway may be a fresh sense of awe at God's creation or a desire to spend more time in His presence in prayer. The point is that you're being changed by what you study. The words you take in through your eyes are finding their way out through your actions.

DIG DEEP

Reading God's Word is an essential first step to growing stronger in your faith—but it's just the beginning. If you really want to grow closer to Christ, you must look for opportunities to apply what you read to your daily life and make reading the Bible a habit. Ask yourself the following questions and answer them truthfully:

1. Do you truly take in what you read and apply it to your life, or are there gray areas that need to change?
2. What questions do you ask to help you apply a passage of Scripture to your life?

◆ DAY 71 ◆

More Bible Passages That Changed My Life

The things you have learned and received and
heard and seen in me, practice these things,
and the God of peace will be with you.
—PHILIPPIANS 4:9

THE POTENTIAL FOR GOD'S WORD TO CHANGE LIVES IS limitless. In an earlier devotion, I shared three passages that had a profound impact on me. But a trio of verses barely scratches the surface. Here are three more Bible passages that transformed my life.

The first is 1 Timothy 6:8: "If we have food and covering, with these we shall be content." The best way to tell if we're truly content is to examine our prayer life. Often, we take a list of our needs and wants to God and wait for Him to furnish them. If He doesn't, we pray harder. If that still doesn't work, we question Him and wonder why He's ignoring us. But the solution may be to shorten our list of needs and wants and ask Him to help us be content with less. If we learn to be content with what God gives us, we will discover a sense of joy and gratitude that transforms the way we look at the world.

The second is James 1:2–4: "Consider it all joy, my brothers and sisters, when you encounter various trials, knowing that the testing of your faith produces endurance. And let endurance have its perfect result, so that you may be perfect and complete, lacking in nothing." James wasn't asking us to trick ourselves into believing that things are great when they're not. He didn't want us to divorce ourselves from reality. And he wasn't asking us to pretend to be joyful to mask our fear or frustration.

Instead, this passage is asking us to trust God's process, to put our faith in His ability to sharpen and strengthen us through adversity. James was asking us to widen our perspective. Obviously, it's important for us to pay attention to the crisis at hand. But it's equally important to anticipate the amazing things that God will do in and through the crisis. Understanding that God sees the big picture and is working in our circumstances is where we find joy.

The third is 2 Timothy 4:2: "Preach the word; be ready in season and out of season; correct, rebuke, and exhort, with great patience and instruction." This passage is a call for us to immerse ourselves in God's Word. To put it at the center of our lives so that it impacts everything we do, say, and think. That's the only way we can be ready to share it "in season and out"—that is, whenever the opportunity arises. We must know what we're talking about. We must learn to share God's truth in ways that will impact others.

—————————————— DIG DEEP ——————————————

The fact that certain Bible passages resonate powerfully with you is part of your unique design. God tuned your heart to a specific biblical frequency. That allows you to minister to people whose hearts are tuned to similar frequencies. Some verses will also mean a lot during a certain season in your life. Ask yourself the following questions and answer them truthfully:

1. What similarities do you see in the Bible passages that have had the biggest impact on you?
2. How do you explain the changes these passages brought about in your life?
3. How can you draw on your own experiences to help others understand and apply God's Word?

DAY 72

Christians and Alcohol

*Do not look at wine when it is red, when it sparkles
in the cup, when it goes down smoothly; in the end
it bites like a snake and stings like a viper.*
—PROVERBS 23:31–32

SOME OF THE MOST HEATED DEBATES AMONG REBORN
believers involve alcohol. Certain denominations teach that alcohol
should be avoided at all costs. Others take a more moderate stance. If
you grew up in the church, it's likely that your attitude toward alcohol today can be traced back to that early influence, whether you
embraced your church's teaching or rebelled against it. But what
does the Bible really say about alcohol? Are Christians allowed to
drink?

First things first: the Bible does not condemn drinking. In fact,
alcohol is featured in a surprising number of Bible passages. Jesus'
first miracle, as recorded in John 2, was to turn water into wine during a wedding celebration. Psalm 104:14–15 celebrates alcohol as part
of God's creation: "He causes the grass to grow for the cattle, and
vegetation for the labor of mankind, so that they may produce food
from the earth, and wine, which makes a human heart cheerful."
And Ecclesiastes 9:7 says, "Go then, eat your bread in happiness, and
drink your wine with a cheerful heart; for God has already approved
your works."

The Bible *does* condemn drunkenness, however. Ephesians 5:18
says, "And do not get drunk with wine, in which there is debauch-
ery, but be filled with the Spirit." And Proverbs 20:1 says, "Wine is a

156

mocker, intoxicating drink a brawler, and whoever is intoxicated by it is not wise."

For many people, including myself, alcohol played a large role in their old nature—the person they used to be before they came to Christ. Peter said, "For the time already past is sufficient for you to have carried out the desire of the Gentiles, having pursued a course of indecent behavior, lusts, drunkenness, carousing, drinking parties, and wanton idolatries" (1 Peter 4:3). For some Christians, the decision not to drink is part of their new identity in Christ, of leaving behind their old nature.

"All things in moderation" seems to be a good rule of thumb when it comes to Christians drinking alcohol. But there's an important exception to that rule, and it's found in Romans 14:13: "Therefore let us not judge one another anymore, but rather determine this: not to put an obstacle or a stumbling block in a brother's or sister's way." We must not be a stumbling block to people who struggle with alcohol. Not everyone has the self-control to enjoy alcohol in moderation. And for some people, alcohol is the cause of untold family misery.

Showing godly love and concern for those people is far more important than exercising our Christian freedom to drink. So even though the Bible doesn't forbid Christians from drinking, sometimes the decision not to drink is the best one.

DIG DEEP

The issue of Christians drinking alcohol (in moderation) comes down to a personal choice. But that choice should be made after considering what the Bible says and praying for God's wisdom and guidance. Ask yourself the following questions and answer them truthfully:

1. What is your attitude toward alcohol?
2. What are some things that influenced or helped shape your attitude?
3. How would you defend your position biblically?

How Does God Speak to Us?

Make me know Your ways, Lord; teach me Your paths.
Lead me in Your truth and teach me, for You are the
God of my salvation; for You I wait all the day.
—Psalm 25:4–5

THE MOMENT WE BECOME A REBORN BELIEVER, WE establish a spiritual relationship with God. We can only worship God in Spirit and truth because God is Spirit (John 4:24). His Spirit in us leads our soul with our own will, intellect, and emotions to build a strong relationship with Him.

This is a special relationship in which the God of the universe knows everything about us and wants us to know everything about Him. As with any relationship, the key to our relationship with God is good communication.

That communication must run two ways. Too often we tell God what we need or what's causing us anxiety and then wait for Him to take care of it. When He does, we thank Him. The communication runs one way, from us to Him.

To open the second line of communication, we need to listen and let God speak to us. God mainly speaks to us in two ways: through the *Logos* and *Rhema*. *Logos* is the written Word of God, which has already been revealed to us. It also refers to Jesus Himself. *Rhema* refers to God's Spirit talking directly to us about a specific thing or occasion in our lives.

God made sure that everything we need to know is in His Word. The Bible is perfect, and we can fully trust what it says. Paul said,

"All Scripture is inspired by God and beneficial for teaching, for rebuke, for correction, for training in righteousness; so that the man or woman of God may be fully capable, equipped for every good work" (2 Timothy 3:16–17).

God speaks to us through the life of His Son. Jesus came to earth not just to save us but to show us how to live. After Jesus ascended to God the Father, He sent us the Holy Spirit to help us. God speaks to us through His Spirit by giving us confirmation, peace, and discernment about certain things when we pray about them. The Holy Spirit can speak to us when we read the Bible, when we go to church, when we talk to brothers and sisters in Christ, when we pray, and when we look at nature or even at the bumper sticker of a car driving by.

If you are not sure if it's God speaking to you, ask Him to confirm it. God called Samuel three times before he listened (1 Samuel 3). When you pray about big things, such as marriage or your career, be patient and trust that God will answer you when the time is right.

Together the Bible and the Holy Spirit are always guiding you, leading you forward in God's purpose and plan for your life. This is how you can live through the Spirit. The Spirit will always guide you to obey God's Word in even the small things you do every day.

DIG DEEP

If you're unsure whether you are hearing God's message correctly, compare it with the Scriptures like the good Bereans: "For they received the word with great eagerness, examining the Scriptures daily to see whether these things were so" (Acts 17:11). Ask yourself the following questions and answer them truthfully:

1. How has God spoken to you in the past?
2. How do you recognize God's voice?

Finding Hope When You're Feeling Hopeless

Let's hold firmly to the confession of our hope without wavering, for He who promised is faithful.
—HEBREWS 10:23

MANY DIFFERENT CIRCUMSTANCES IN LIFE THREATEN TO steal our hope and joy. It could be a major, life-changing loss, diagnosis, or tragedy. Or it could be several smaller "thieves"—the daily grind of life, dissatisfaction in our job or a relationship, loneliness, financial strain, periodic struggles with depression or anxiety—that gradually take away little pieces of our optimism and well-being, until we're left with next to nothing. Even for reborn believers, the resulting sense of hopelessness can sometimes seem like too much to bear.

Paul said, "No temptation has overtaken you except something common to mankind; and God is faithful, so He will not allow you to be tempted beyond what you are able, but with the temptation will provide the way of escape also, so that you will be able to endure it" (1 Corinthians 10:13). We can overcome hope-robbing situations because we don't live by our feelings; we live by the truth and promises of God. We may be tempted to lose hope, but God will not allow us to be pushed that far. Real hope from God is the assurance that He will keep His promises.

When we struggle with feelings of hopelessness, we must look up. It's tempting to keep our eyes focused on the causes of our hopelessness. But Psalm 121:1–2 says, "I will raise my eyes to the mountains; from where will my help come? My help comes from the LORD, who made heaven and earth."

Instead of looking at the obstacles that block hope in our lives, we must look to the One who can clear away the obstacles. No problem, setback, or tragedy on earth is bigger than the Lord who made heaven and earth.

The trap we fall into is trying to deal with hopelessness based on our own understanding of it. Proverbs 3:5–6 says, "Trust in the LORD with all your heart and do not lean on your own understanding. In all your ways acknowledge Him, and He will make your paths straight."

When we live by what we see and not by faith, we can see and feel the things that rob us of our hope, but we can't always see or feel God's work of resupplying us with hope. We must trust Him and have faith in His unseen work. Paul said, "Therefore we do not lose heart, but though our outer person is decaying, yet our inner person is being renewed day by day. For momentary, light affliction is producing for us an eternal weight of glory far beyond all comparison, while we look not at the things which are seen, but at the things which are not seen; for the things which are seen are temporal, but the things which are not seen are eternal" (2 Corinthians 4:16–18).

DIG DEEP

Peter encouraged reborn believers to "always [be] ready to make a defense to everyone who asks you to give an account for the hope that is in you" (1 Peter 3:15). Hope is a given for God's people. Ask yourself the following questions and answer them truthfully:

1. How do you access and protect that hope?
2. How can you help others find hope?

How to Know If You're
Really Saved

*These things I have written to you who believe in the name of
the Son of God, so that you may know that you have eternal life.*
—1 John 5:13

IF YOU'VE EVER EXPERIENCED A SERIOUS TRAVEL MIX-UP,
you know the dangers of depending on guarantees when it comes to
airline reservations or hotel bookings. You arrive at the counter, fully
expecting to be admitted, only to discover that whatever you did to
gain admittance wasn't enough.

That uncertainty is a minor annoyance when you travel. But if
you have that same kind of uncertainty about eternal life, it can be
devastating. It's hard to grow and thrive in the Christian life if you
constantly need reassurance that Christ did indeed save you. If you
struggle with guilt, you may think of it in different terms, wondering
if you've done something to lose your salvation.

John anticipated those doubts and questions. As he said in the
passage above, that's why he wrote his first letter—"So that you may
know." Not *hope,* not *wonder,* but *know.*

Here's what you need to understand. Giving your life to Christ
involves much more than believing that God exists or that Jesus loves
you. It involves admitting that you're a sinner who deserves God's
wrath. It involves recognizing that no amount of good works can
save you, that only Jesus' sacrifice can pay the price for your sin. It
involves asking God to forgive you and to cover your sins with the
blood of Jesus.

When you do that, God's Holy Spirit takes up residence inside you, transforms you, and seals you until the day of redemption. He frees you from your old nature and gives you a new nature. God also gives you assurance of eternal life with Him.

The reality of your faith is evident in your changed life. Your priorities, attitude, actions, and relationships reflect your desire to be like Christ. There will be times when you stumble. But even they will reflect your changed nature because you'll feel an urgent sense of wanting to restore your relationship with Christ.

But what you need to understand is that those occasional stumbles have no bearing on your salvation. Paul said, "For I am confident of this very thing, that He who began a good work among you will complete it by the day of Christ Jesus" (Philippians 1:6).

Your salvation doesn't depend on you. You cannot become a true reborn Christian on your own because the promise of eternal life isn't based on anything you do. Jesus' words in John 10:28 give you all the assurance you'll ever need: "I give them eternal life, and they will never perish; and no one will snatch them out of My hand."

DIG DEEP

If you are a reborn believer, nothing can change your status before God. Eternal life is promised to you by the Lord, who always keeps His promises. Ask yourself the following questions and answer them truthfully:

1. Why does God want you to be sure of your salvation?
2. Why does the devil want you to question your salvation?
3. What can you do when you start to worry about whether you are saved?

Winning the Battle Against Temptation

Submit therefore to God. But resist the devil and he will flee from you.

—JAMES 4:7

SOME PEOPLE MISTAKENLY ASSUME THAT TEMPTATION lessens when we become reborn believers. But that's not the case. In fact, Satan steps up his attacks to stunt our Christian growth and limit our impact for Christ. We can give in to temptation such as food, pornography, money, alcohol, or just about anything else that appeals to us.

Jesus Himself was tempted. Matthew 4 tells how, after Jesus spent forty days in the wilderness fasting, Satan appeared to Him. Taking advantage of Jesus' weakened state, Satan offered Him three enticing, hard-to-resist temptations. This is one example of why the writer of Hebrews could confidently say this about Jesus: "For we do not have a high priest who cannot sympathize with our weaknesses, but One who has been tempted in all things just as we are, yet without sin" (Hebrews 4:15).

Yet without sin. That's the legacy Jesus left us. He is the only person ever to go undefeated by temptation. And in His encounter with Satan we see His simple but effective strategy for resisting temptation. And it's one that will work for us as well.

Three times Satan tempted Jesus, and three times Jesus immediately quoted Scripture in response. Let's start with the "immediately" part. Jesus didn't stop to think about what Satan was offering. He didn't weigh the pros and cons of giving in to temptation. He didn't try to minimize the damage it would cause. He didn't wrestle with whether the end justified the means. In other words, He didn't give temptation a foothold in His life. As soon as temptation presented itself, He turned it away.

That's what we must do: reject temptation immediately. If we give it room in our thoughts, it will start to look more attractive. And in a moment of weakness, we may give in. But if we push it out of our minds as soon as it appears, we won't have to worry about it.

The other aspect of Jesus' strategy was quoting God's Word. If you know the Bible, you know the truth and the truth will set you free. The Word of God is like a two-edged sword (Hebrews 4:12); the more you know the truth, the better you will be able to use it for spiritual warfare and cut through any lie Satan throws at you.

Every time Satan presented a temptation, Jesus had just the right Scripture passage to counter him. Notice that Satan didn't try to argue with Scripture. After the third try he left, thoroughly defeated. If Satan succeeds in shifting your focus away from the truth of God's Word and toward your own emotions or what other people say, he's got you.

God's Word is the key to defeating Satan and his temptations. So it's essential that we learn to use it effectively. We do that by spending time in it daily, by studying passages that speak to the situations we face, by committing key verses to memory, and by building our lives according to its truths.

DIG DEEP

Scripture says, "God is faithful, and he will not let you be tempted beyond your ability" (1 Corinthians 10:13). Ask yourself the following questions and answer them truthfully:

1. Which temptations are hardest for you to resist?
2. What would a victory over temptation look like in your life?

Sharing Your Faith
Telling Your Story

*Whether He is a sinner, I do not know; one thing I
do know, that though I was blind, now I see.*
—John 9:25

AFTER JESUS HEALED A MAN WHO HAD BEEN BLIND
since birth, His enemies, the Pharisees, tried to discredit Him. They
claimed that Jesus was a sinner and therefore incapable of perform-
ing such a miracle. They tried to enlist the healed man into their
disinformation campaign. His reply is found in the passage above.

The man had a story to tell about a personal encounter with
Jesus. His story resonated with people and caused them to rethink
their opinions of the rabbi from Nazareth. And there was nothing
Jesus' enemies could do to prevent that. This shows us not only the
power of Jesus but also the power of a personal narrative. If you
have a story about an encounter with Jesus, you have the potential
to make a difference in others' lives. (And if you're a reborn believer,
you *do* have a story to tell.) Here are a few ways to harness your
story's potential.

Capture it. Spend some time thinking about the person you were
before you came to Christ and the person you are now. What differences do you see? How did you get from point A to point B? Paul
said, "Therefore if anyone is in Christ, this person is a new creature; the old things passed away; behold, new things have come"
(2 Corinthians 5:17). Capturing your story means finding a way to
describe that process.

Celebrate it. Your story tells about God's work in your life. Give thanks for it constantly. Find joy in it. You may discover that others will celebrate with you because joy is contagious. Proverbs 10:28 says, "The hope of the righteous is gladness."

Don't underestimate it. Your story has the potential to impact others. Resist the urge to embellish it. Don't try to compete with people who have more dramatic or compelling stories to tell. You never know who will connect with the relatable details of your experience. You never know who will see themselves in you.

Practice it. Learn to tell your story in a way that holds people's attention. You don't necessarily want it to seem scripted, but practice does make perfect. The more comfortable you are with telling your story, the better it will come across. The best way to do this is through trial and error. People are also different, so pay attention to how different types of people react to your story, and then make changes accordingly.

Share it. If you have personally experienced the truth of Psalm 100:5—"The LORD is good; His mercy is everlasting and His faithfulness to all generations"—people need to hear from you. They need to know that they can experience it too.

DIG DEEP

If Christ has made a difference in your life, it's selfish to keep that to yourself. If we love others as we love ourselves, then we want them to be saved as well. Ask yourself the following questions and answer them truthfully:

1. What is your story and how many times have you told it in the last year?
2. Who among your circle of acquaintances needs to hear it?
3. How can you tell it most effectively?

Sharing Your Faith
Preparing to Answer Questions

Sanctify Christ as Lord in your hearts, always being ready to make a defense to everyone who asks you to give an account for the hope that is in you, yet with gentleness and respect.
—1 Peter 3:15

WOULDN'T IT BE GREAT IF WE COULD GET ADVANCE notice that someone would be asking a question about the Christian faith before they ask it? Unfortunately, that's not how things work. In reality, if a question occurs to someone, they usually ask it. If they hear something they don't agree with, they object—whether reborn believers are ready or not.

That's why Peter gave the instructions in the passage above. He spoke from experience. Matthew 26 tells us that on the night Jesus was arrested, Peter was recognized as one of His disciples. Peter had an opportunity to talk about the amazing things he'd heard and seen during his time with Jesus. But he wasn't prepared. Not only did Peter miss his opportunity, but he denied that he even knew Jesus.

If we're not prepared to defend our faith or to offer reasons for our spiritual hope in all situations, we'll miss valuable opportunities. Yes, the idea of defending or even explaining the Christian faith can be intimidating to those of us who aren't Bible scholars or to those who are not in the habit of sharing the gospel. But it should not be that way. The truth of the gospel doesn't depend on our ability to answer every question immediately and perfectly. The key is to address the motive or driving force of the person behind the question.

There are ways to prepare. The first is *daily Bible study*, continuously working to understand God's Word. When we come across passages that we think might speak to unbelievers, we can write them in our journal, along with some notes that will help us explain them.

The second is *consultation*. We can talk to Christian leaders and mature believers about certain difficult questions to find out how they answer them. We can ask them for advice on how to be effective defenders of the faith.

The third is *prayer*. We can take our questions and concerns to God. We can ask Him to help us understand difficult concepts. We can ask for His guidance and direction when we talk to others about our faith. We must rely on the Holy Spirit in us to help and guide us at all times, because if we do it through our flesh, we will fail every time.

Peter challenged us to answer questions "with gentleness and respect." Some people who are hostile to the Christian faith may try to coax us into an angry confrontation. But as Solomon said, "A gentle answer turns away wrath, but a harsh word stirs up anger" (Proverbs 15:1). If we maintain a gentle and respectful attitude, our words will have more of an impact.

Always remember, it is not just what you say but how you say it.

DIG DEEP

Being prepared to defend your faith doesn't mean you'll have all the answers. If you don't have an answer, say so—and then do your best to find one. Ask yourself the following questions and answer them truthfully:

1. What questions did you have about the Christian faith before you became a reborn believer?
2. What questions do you feel unprepared to answer?
3. How will you share the gospel with an atheist, a Hindu, a Muslim, a Buddhist, or a spiritualist?

Sharing Your Faith
Living Your Witness

I have been crucified with Christ; and it is no longer
I who live, but Christ lives in me; and the life which
I now live in the flesh I live by faith in the Son of
God, who loved me and gave Himself up for me.
—GALATIANS 2:20

"PREACH THE GOSPEL AT ALL TIMES. USE WORDS IF necessary." This well-known saying may exaggerate the point a little. After all, as reborn believers, we cannot share the truth if we do not speak the truth. But it gets to the heart of many people's reactions to Christians sharing our faith. That is, they pay more attention to reborn believers who walk the walk instead of just talking the talk. To put it another way, unbelievers are more likely to listen to what we say after they've watched what we do.

That's fair. Because if the gospel of Christ is truly life-changing, as we claim it is, then it's reasonable to expect to see unmistakable evidence of it in the way we live. To open the door of evangelism, we need to live in such a way that people recognize something different in us—something that's appealing, something that's worth investigating, and something that's missing in their lives. A bright light that those who live in darkness cannot resist.

We need to bring Matthew 5:14–16 to life: "You are the light of the world. A city set on a hill cannot be hidden; nor do people light a lamp and put it under a basket, but on the lampstand, and it gives light to all who are in the house. Your light must shine before people in such a way that they may see your good works, and glorify your Father who is in heaven."

Those good works should be apparent in our lives not because we want to get credit for them but because we want to follow Christ's example of serving others. If we make it a priority to meet the needs of the people around us—to love our neighbors as ourselves—we'll find plenty of opportunities to share our faith.

In sharing our faith, words without actions are empty. On the other hand, actions without words can't explain the gift of salvation and the life-changing potential of making Jesus Lord. Living in a godly way may get the attention of people who otherwise wouldn't be interested in Christianity. But once we have their attention, we need to be prepared to talk in truth and in love.

DIG DEEP

James said, "What use is it, my brothers and sisters, if someone says he has faith, but he has no works? Can that faith save him? If a brother or sister is without clothing and in need of daily food, and one of you says to them, 'Go in peace, be warmed and be filled,' yet you do not give them what is necessary for their body, what use is that?" (James 2:14–16). The good works that result from your faith in Christ can lead other people to Christ. That gives you an amazing opportunity and a worthwhile challenge every day. Ask yourself the following questions and answer them truthfully:

1. Whose example of living the Christian faith had an impact on you?
2. What does living your witness look like in your life?
3. How would you respond to someone who observed, "There's something different about you"?

Sharing Your Faith
Explaining What the Bible Says

Philip . . . said, "Do you understand what you are reading?"
And he said, "Well, how could I, unless someone guides me?"
—ACTS 8:30–31

SHARING OUR FAITH BEGINS WITH GOD'S WORD. EVEN the most dynamic outreach strategy is meaningless if it's not based on Scripture. Jesus said in John 8:31–32, "If you continue in My word, then you are truly My disciples; and you will know the truth, and the truth will set you free."

When we present the gospel to unbelievers, we must help them understand a few key biblical truths. First, *God is holy and just*. "For You are not a God who takes pleasure in wickedness; no evil can dwell with You" (Psalm 5:4). He is completely separate from sin and demands punishment for it as a righteous Judge.

Second, *God gave us free will*. He could have created us to obey Him and made it part of our DNA. Instead, He gave us a choice. Adam and Eve had the option of obeying or disobeying Him in the garden of Eden. We have the same option.

Third, *our sin separated us from God and made us subject to His punishment, which is death*. "For the wages of sin is death, but the gracious gift of God is eternal life in Christ Jesus our Lord" (Romans 6:23).

Fourth, *as sinners, we can do nothing to save ourselves from God's punishment*. "For by grace you have been saved through faith; and this is not of yourselves, it is the gift of God; not as a result of works, so that no one may boast" (Ephesians 2:8–9).

Fifth, *instead of punishing us like we deserve, God loved us so much that He sent His Son to save us.* Jesus came in human form to live a sinless life so He could become the sacrifice God required and take the punishment for our sin. "For God so loved the world, that He gave His only Son, so that everyone who believes in Him will not perish, but have eternal life" (John 3:16).

Sixth, *Jesus was crucified for our sins and then rose from the dead to conquer death once and for all.* "Our Savior Christ Jesus . . . abolished death and brought life and immortality to light through the gospel" (2 Timothy 1:10).

Seventh, *Jesus is the only way to God.* Jesus said, "I am the way, and the truth, and the life; no one comes to the Father except through Me" (John 14:6). Anyone who believes in Jesus will have eternal life.

These biblical truths are the building blocks of evangelism. They are the basic Christian concepts a spiritually hungry world needs to hear. It's important that we explain them even if some reject the truth.

DIG DEEP

Jesus said, "The Holy Spirit . . . will teach you all things, and remind you of all that I said to you" (John 14:26). If you're faithful in sharing the gospel from Scripture, the Holy Spirit will guide your words and help them impact people's lives. Ask yourself the following questions and answer them truthfully:

1. When was the last time you shared the gospel with someone?
2. What are some effective ways of introducing Scripture into your daily conversations?
3. How can you become more comfortable with sharing God's Word?

Winning the Battle Against Porn

Now flee from youthful lusts and pursue
righteousness, faith, love, and peace with those
who call on the Lord from a pure heart.
—2 TIMOTHY 2:22

LUST IS ONE OF SATAN'S MOST DANGEROUS WEAPONS. And thanks to the internet, it's become even more dangerous. It's estimated that porn sites record more monthly users than Netflix, Amazon, and Twitter combined. Many underage human trafficking victims reported being exploited online through porn. Lust is anything but a victimless crime.

Despite the evidence, some people still downplay the dangers of lust and porn. Jesus was not one of them. He said, "You have heard that it was said, 'You shall not commit adultery'; but I say to you that everyone who looks at a woman with lust for her has already committed adultery with her in his heart. Now if your right eye is causing you to sin, tear it out and throw it from you; for it is better for you to lose one of the parts of your body, than for your whole body to be thrown into hell" (Matthew 5:27–29). He treated lust as the serious sin it is.

The good news is that it is possible to win the battle against lust. The Bible tells us how. First, *we need to confess our struggle.* We need to bring it into the light instead of hiding it in the dark, where it festers and grows. Proverbs 28:13 says, "One who conceals his wrongdoings will not prosper, but one who confesses and abandons them will find compassion."

Second, *we need to run away.* Paul said, "Flee sexual immorality" (1 Corinthians 6:18). Other passages encourage us to "stand firm in the faith" (including 1 Corinthians 16:13). Lust can be triggered by just a glimpse. And once it starts it can be difficult to stop.

One way to flee is by identifying situations in which we're likely to look at porn. Knowing our triggers can help us avoid them. We can limit our access by installing search engine blocks. Instead of trying to resist temptation later, we can prevent it now.

Third, *we need to read God's Word.* Paul said, "[Take] up the shield of faith with which you will be able to extinguish all the flaming arrows of the evil one. And take . . . the sword of the Spirit, which is the word of God" (Ephesians 6:16–17). The battle against lust isn't just physical; it's also spiritual. Growing stronger in our faith gives us the power to break lust's hold on us. When we act through the flesh, we will fall, but when we act through the Spirit, we will overcome temptation and sin. That power comes from studying and living the truth of Scripture. God's Word changes the way we think, act, and fight, and it gives us victory over sin.

DIG DEEP

Even if you don't struggle with porn yourself, you probably know someone who does. Ask yourself the following questions and answer them truthfully:

1. Are you struggling with lust?
2. What does fleeing lust look like in your life?
3. How can you overcome this sin or help someone who may be struggling with lust or porn?

What If You Died Today?

DAY 82

What If You Died Today?

*"I am the resurrection and the life; the one who believes
in Me will live, even if he dies, and everyone who lives
and believes in Me will never die. Do you believe this?"*
—John 11:25–26

ON AVERAGE, AROUND 333,000 PEOPLE DIE EVERY DAY.
We don't know when we'll be part of that statistic. James said, "Yet
you do not know what your life will be like tomorrow. You are just a
vapor that appears for a little while, and then vanishes away" (James
4:14).

We can't take life for granted, and we can't ignore what comes
next. Hebrews 9:27 says, "It is destined for people to die once and
after this comes judgment." Every one of us will face judgment when
we die, and this reality needs to sink in so that we will be prepared
for it. Most of us like to believe that we're good people, that the
things we've done right in this world outweigh the things we've done
wrong. And we have a list of good works to prove the point.

To that, Isaiah would say, "All of us have become like one who is
unclean, and all our righteous deeds are like a filthy garment" (Isaiah
64:6). All the good works in the world are not good enough and cannot save us. Only Jesus can.

Ephesians 2:8–10 says, "For by grace you have been saved through
faith; and this is not of yourselves, it is the gift of God; not as a result
of works, so that no one may boast. For we are His workmanship,
created in Christ Jesus for good works, which God prepared before-
hand so that we would walk in them." Putting our faith in Christ is

176

the only way to escape eternal punishment when we die. After we put our faith in Christ, our good works are evidence of our faith.

To prepare for the end of this life, we must first make sure that we will spend our next life in God's presence forever. Second, we must live each day according to God's will, and that includes sharing the gospel. I have met many Christians who told me after the death of a loved one that the one thing they regret most is not effectively sharing the good news of Jesus with their loved one. It is selfish to think only of our own salvation and not use the time that we are given to share the gospel with those around us.

What an incredible relief it is to be able to say, as Paul did, "For I am convinced that neither death, nor life, nor angels, nor principalities, nor things present, nor things to come, nor powers, nor height, nor depth, nor any other created thing will be able to separate us from the love of God, which is in Christ Jesus our Lord" (Romans 8:38–39).

DIG DEEP

Paul said, "Death has been swallowed up in victory" (1 Corinthians 15:54). If you believe in Christ, you have no reason to fear death. Ask yourself the following questions and answer them truthfully:

1. How can you know that you will go to be with Christ when you die?
2. Are you using your time to truthfully and lovingly share the gospel with your loved ones, or are you more concerned about this temporary world, while their souls may be lost forever?

The Truth About Angels

Do not neglect hospitality to strangers, for by this
some have entertained angels without knowing it.
—Hebrews 13:2

YOU CAN FIND ANGELS ON TV, IN THE MOVIES, ON PRODUCT
labels, on clothes, on bumper stickers, and as decorations. Contrary
to what some people (even Christians!) say, humans do not become
angels when they die. Humans are created in the image of God and
will receive their eternal bodies when they live in the new heaven
and the new earth. But who are angels and what do they do? For
answers, we must turn to God's Word.

First, *angels are powerful creatures created by God.* Psalm 103:20
says, "Bless the LORD, you His angels, mighty in strength, who
perform His word, obeying the voice of His word!" But they're not
all-powerful. Only God is almighty; He is El Shaddai. Angels are in
the presence of God and have a more complete view of God and His
work than we do. But only God is all-knowing; He is El De'ot. Angels
were created by God and are eternal spirits (Luke 20:36).

Angels answer to the Creator. They go where He sends them,
do what He instructs, and deliver the messages He gives them. Yet
they were created with free will, just as we were. They can choose to
serve and obey God or not. Satan and his demonic followers chose to
rebel and will suffer the consequences for all eternity.

Second, looking at biblical history, *angels played a role in key
moments.* In Genesis 18 they announced that Abraham and Sarah
would have a child, even though the couple was very old. In

1 Kings 19, an angel fed and comforted Elijah. In Daniel 6, an angel held the mouths of hungry lions closed to protect Daniel. In Luke 2, an angel announced the birth of Jesus to a group of shepherds. In Acts 5 and 12, an angel released Peter from prison. All these angels weren't acting on their own. Psalm 103:21 makes it clear that angels serve the Lord, "doing His will."

Third, *angels are working-class heavenly beings*. Because of the incredible nature of some angelic appearances in Scripture, people sometimes give angels more credit than they deserve. In fact, angel worship was a common practice in biblical times.

The author of Hebrews compared Christ and angels to prove that Christ is superior. In Hebrews 1:6, the heavenly Father says of His Son, "Let all the angels of God worship Him." That's the true order of things. Angels do the worshiping; Christ receives the worship.

Angels are God's messengers, His servants. They don't protect us; God protects us. They don't watch over us; God watches over us. They don't guide us; God guides us. The fact that angels are involved in those efforts shouldn't divert our attention from the One who is ultimately responsible for our well-being.

—————————————— **DIG DEEP** ——————————————

Angels play important roles in God's work. But God alone deserves the glory for it. Ask yourself the following questions and answer them truthfully:

1. What are some false beliefs about angels that you've heard?
2. Why do some people give angels glory that rightfully belongs to God?

Christians and Gambling

All things are permitted for me, but not all things
are of benefit. All things are permitted for me,
but I will not be mastered by anything.
—1 Corinthians 6:12

MILLIONS OF PEOPLE ALL OVER THE WORLD ARE EITHER addicted to gambling or would admit that gambling interferes with their family, work, and social life. People can get addicted to any number of things, including food, which leads to the sin of gluttony.

Christians face two questions when it comes to gambling. First, *is it wrong?* No Bible verses specifically forbid reborn believers from gambling when it comes to casual wagers in a hobby or competition. But gambling is definitely wrong when we are greedy for more money, when we start to rely on luck instead of relying on God and being content with what He gives us. Hebrews 13:5 says, "Make sure that your character is free from the love of money, being content with what you have."

Paul said, "For the love of money is a root of all sorts of evil, and some by longing for it have wandered away from the faith and pierced themselves with many griefs" (1 Timothy 6:10). The love of money clouds people's judgment, sows seeds of addiction, ruins lives, and destroys families.

God wants us to work for our food instead of being lazy. We see that He is against those who depend on luck to gain wealth: "But as for you who abandon the LORD, who forget My holy mountain, who set a table for Fortune, and who fill a jug of mixed wine for

Destiny, . . . the Lord God will put you to death" (Isaiah 65:11, 15). The Hebrew word used for "fortune" in this passage is *Gad*, meaning "luck."

The second question we must answer about gambling is this: *Is it wise?* Organized gambling—through casinos, online betting sites, and lottery drawings—is designed to rake in enormous amounts of money while paying out next to nothing in comparison. If we choose to play, we're practically guaranteed to lose more than we make. Not only that, but if we choose to gamble, we help these companies stay in business, tempting people who struggle with a gambling addiction to keep on sinning.

How does that line up with Paul's words in Ephesians 5:15: "So then, be careful how you walk, not as unwise people but as wise"? Or with Solomon's words in Proverbs 13:11: "Wealth obtained from nothing dwindles, but the one who gathers by labor increases it"?

Casual wagers between friends can be harmless. There's nothing wrong with adding a little financial incentive to a weekly golf game or collecting a winner-take-all pot for catching the most fish during a weekend getaway. It's harmless fun for anyone who can afford to do it because it relies on skill and not on luck.

Self-control is the key. Paul said self-control is evidence of the Holy Spirit's presence in the life of a believer. And Solomon said, "Like a city that is broken into and without walls so is a person who has no self-control over his spirit" (Proverbs 25:28).

DIG DEEP

If you aren't sure about gambling, ask the Holy Spirit to guide your decision-making in this area. Ask yourself the following questions and answer them truthfully:

1. What is your responsibility as a reborn believer when it comes to gambling?
2. Are you a stumbling block for others if you gamble?

Understanding Paul

For this I was appointed a preacher and an
apostle (I am telling the truth, I am not lying) as
a teacher of the Gentiles in faith and truth.
—1 Timothy 2:7

PAUL IS ONE OF THE MOST IMPORTANT PEOPLE IN Christian history. He wrote most of the New Testament! So it may come as a shock when some say that he was a false apostle or false teacher. Before he became a Christian, Paul was a reborn believer's worst nightmare. As a zealous leader of the Jewish faith, he tried to wipe out Christianity, which he considered a dangerous cult. He dragged Christians away from their homes and put them in prison.

The direction of Paul's life changed forever when Jesus appeared to him while he was traveling. He began preaching the message that he had tried so hard to discredit. Acts 9:21 describes the reaction: "All those hearing him continued to be amazed, and were saying, 'Is this not the one who in Jerusalem destroyed those who called on this name, and had come here for the purpose of bringing them bound before the chief priests?'"

Paul's former Jewish colleagues plotted to have him killed. The hunter became the hunted. After his conversion, Paul reached out to the disciples, but they were still afraid of him. A respected Christian leader named Barnabas intervened and brought them together. The disciples accepted Paul as one of them, and together they shared the gospel boldly (Acts 9:26–28).

Peter later wrote, "Just as also our beloved brother Paul, according to the wisdom given him, wrote to you, as also in all his letters, speaking in them of these things, in which there are some things that are hard to understand, which the untaught and unstable distort, as they do also the rest of the Scriptures, to their own destruction" (2 Peter 3:15–16). Peter made three very important points: (1) Paul's writings are God's Word. (2) Parts of Paul's writings are hard to understand because he was a highly educated Jew who knew the Old Testament. Paul clearly understood the prophecies Jesus fulfilled as the Messiah and how this truth caused the transition from the old covenant to the new. (3) People who don't understand Scripture as well as Paul will twist his words and accuse him of being a false teacher.

People who twist Paul's words show their own spiritual ignorance. Paul's words were inspired by God and are essential for anyone who is serious about their walk with Christ.

Like Paul, we will be persecuted for our faith. We see the war on Christianity everywhere, especially on social media, in the mass media, and in our schools. Good is called evil and evil is called good. But just like Paul we need to keep our eyes fixed on Jesus and stand firm in our faith. We need to put on the whole armor of God at all times and move forward in boldness, truth, and love!

DIG DEEP

Paul was not a false prophet. He was an uncompromising servant of Christ who spoke and wrote God's truth. Ask yourself the following questions and answer them truthfully:

1. How do Peter's words argue against people who say Paul was a false teacher?
2. How would you respond to someone who called Paul a false teacher?

Understanding God
What Nature and Scripture Tell Us

For since the creation of the world His invisible attributes,
that is, His eternal power and divine nature, have been
clearly perceived, being understood through what
has been made, so that they are without excuse.
—ROMANS 1:20

CHRISTIANS BELIEVE GOD EXISTS. BUT THAT HARDLY makes us unique. Millions of demons also believe God is real, but that does not help them. James said, "You believe that God is one. You do well; the demons also believe, and shudder" (James 2:19). What sets reborn believers apart is our faith in Him as Lord and Savior, and our desire to know God, discover what He's like, grow closer to Him, and develop a personal relationship with Him.

The fact that we can even hope to know anything about the Supreme Being of the universe is because God has made it possible. He has taken the initiative in revealing Himself to us. Without His self-revelation we would be clueless about what God is really like.

God makes Himself known to us in three ways: through nature, through His Word, and through personal experience. In this devotion, we're going to look at the first two.

Let's start with nature. God created the universe. We know this because the Bible says so (Genesis 1:1) and because He left His fingerprints all over His work. By looking at the world around us, we can find clues as to what the Creator is like.

When we see an awesome natural wonder, such as Victoria Falls or the Grand Canyon, and realize that God spoke it into existence, we get a sense of His power. When we see the stunning spectacle of the Painted Desert, or even just a sunset, we get a sense of His appreciation of beauty. When we see the complex design of the human body or the amazing ways in which living creatures are connected, we get a sense of His perfect design.

Nature gives us a general sense of what God is like. The Bible gives us a much more accurate picture. In fact, everything God wants us to know about Him can be found in His Word. Let's start with the name He chose for Himself in Exodus 3:14: "I AM." These two words may seem vague ("I am" . . . what?), but they give us a perfect starting point for exploring who God is. God is saying, "No matter what else seems real or logical to you, I am."

Others pretend; God is. Other things "give the appearance of"; God is. Others claim; God is. Some were, some are, and some will be; God is. So when we answer the question, *What is God like?* the only information we can rely on is what comes from I AM Himself.

In the Bible, we see evidence of God's character in His interactions with people. We discover His priorities through His commandments and punishments. We see His incredible plan in His prophecies and His intervention in human events. We see it all because God has made Himself known to us.

DIG DEEP

God has revealed Himself to you. Your best response is to learn as much about Him as you can. Ask yourself the following questions and answer them truthfully:

1. What does nature reveal to you about God?
2. What does Scripture reveal to you about God?
3. When was the last time you thanked God for revealing Himself to you?

Understanding God
What Our Personal Encounters Tell Us

The secret of the LORD is for those who fear Him,
and He will make them know His covenant.
—PSALM 25:14

GOD REVEALS HIMSELF THROUGH HIS WORD, AND HE reveals Himself through His creation. Sometimes He interrupts our daily routine to show us who He is and what He wants from us.

Most of us can think of at least one experience that can be explained only by God's work, whether it's a perfectly timed, unexpected source of income; an injury or sickness that should have been more serious than it was; or some other answer to prayer. One of the biggest miracles I experienced was when God saved me from death when I was electrocuted. Considering the laws of nature, I should have been dead, but God saved me for a few different reasons.

Sometimes God wants us to experience His power and love in an incredibly personal, unforgettable way. The experience strengthens our faith and equips us to testify about Him to others. However, we need to recognize that God is working not just in the "big things" but also in the small details of our lives. A good example of this is found in 1 Kings 19.

The prophet Elijah was depressed and scared because he thought he was going to be killed for doing God's work. To lift Elijah's spirit, God told him to stand on Mount Horeb. The Lord Himself "was passing by" (verse 11).

While Elijah watched, a powerful wind tore the mountain apart and shattered the rocks around him. Elijah looked for God in the wind, but He wasn't there. Next came a devastating earthquake that shook the mountain to its core. Elijah looked for God in the earthquake, but He wasn't there.

After the earthquake came a roaring fire that consumed everything in its path. Elijah looked for God in the fire, but He wasn't there. Elijah witnessed three powerful natural phenomena—three dramatic events that seemed to have God's revelation written all over them. But that's not how God revealed Himself in this case. And it's not how He reveals Himself most of the time.

As the fire's roar died down, Elijah heard "a sound of a gentle blowing" (verse 12). Verse 13 says, "When Elijah heard it, he wrapped his face in his cloak and went out and stood in the entrance of the cave. And behold, a voice came to him." God was there, in the gentle voice. If Elijah had focused only on the big, dramatic things, he would have missed an unforgettable experience with God.

The same thing goes for us. If we're constantly looking for something dramatic, we're going to miss many important revelations from God. We need to look carefully at the things that go on in our lives and search for evidence of God's work, guidance, and love. His gentle voice tells us what He is like.

DIG DEEP

Celebrate God when He makes Himself known to you in an unmistakable way. But don't miss the gentle voice He uses the rest of the time. Ask yourself the following questions and answer them truthfully:

1. How has God made Himself known to you in an unmistakable way?
2. How can you keep your ears tuned to God's voice?

Understanding God
His Perfections

The LORD is righteous in all His ways, and kind in all His works.
—PSALM 145:17

THE MOST IMPORTANT THING GOD REVEALS ABOUT Himself in Scripture are His perfections. We refer to other people's qualities as "characteristics" or "personality traits," but those words don't apply to God. When we use adjectives like "caring," "impatient," or "funny" to describe people, we're talking in general terms. No one is caring all the time or making people laugh all the time. We understand that a person can be a little this and a little that.

But that's not the case with God. He's not "somewhat" merciful; His mercy is perfect. He doesn't "become" just, depending on the circumstances; His justice is complete. He isn't "kind of" loving; His love is the standard that all other love is measured against because God is love.

His perfections are always in complete harmony. For example, His love never gets in the way of His justice. He is always completely loving and completely just. If that seems impossible, it's because we human beings don't have the brainpower to fully understand God. Our only option is to take Him at His word when He describes Himself. Let's look at five ways God describes Himself in Scripture.

God is eternal. There's never been a time when He didn't exist, and there will never be a time when He doesn't exist. Psalm 90:1–2 says, "Lord, You have been our dwelling place in all generations. Before the mountains were born or You gave birth to the earth and the world, even from everlasting to everlasting, You are God." That's why we can trust His promises to *always* be with us.

God is holy. Sin cannot exist in His presence because everything about Him is good and right. Everything He does is good because He does it. Everything He commands is the right thing to do because He commands it. If we do what He says, it will always be the right thing.

God is immanent. He is intimately involved with His creation. He's right here with us, always present, always near. We have access to Him around the clock. When He says, "I am with you" (Isaiah 41:10), He means, "No matter where you go or what you do, I will be there."

God is just. Habakkuk 1:13 says, "Your eyes are too pure to look at evil, and You can not look at harm favorably." Because God is just, He cannot allow sin to go unpunished. That's why Jesus had to die in our place: to take the punishment that God demands for our sin.

God is loving. God's love is perfect, and perfect love involves instruction, correction, discipline, and allowing us to face the consequences of our actions. Hebrews 12:6 says, "For whom the Lord loves He disciplines." He wants only what's best for us and will do what needs to be done to make sure we pursue it. God's love also makes it possible for us to love others.

DIG DEEP

Every perfection of God is complete in Him, all the time. He's not holy one day and loving the next. Understanding how His perfections coexist is one of the most rewarding challenges you'll ever face. Ask yourself the following questions and answer them truthfully:

1. How can you be holy as God is holy?
2. What does God's constant presence look like in your life?
3. How do you balance God's justice and love in your understanding of Him?

Understanding God
More of His Perfections

Great is our Lord and abundant in strength;
His understanding is infinite.
—PSALM 147:5

GOD IS ETERNAL, HOLY, IMMANENT, JUST, AND LOVING. But those perfections capture only part of who He is and what He's like, according to Scripture. Let's look at five other perfections that give us a more complete image of our heavenly Father.

God is omnipotent. God can do anything that is in His nature. His power over the universe is limitless. He can override the rules that govern the natural world. The Bible contains story after story of His miraculous interventions. God's omnipotence and love are a great combination for those who love Him. The same hands that held back the Red Sea now hold us in their grasp, and no one can snatch us out of them. That's why Paul was so confident when he said, "I am convinced that [nothing] . . . will be able to separate us from the love of God" (Romans 8:38–39).

God is omniscient. He knows everything that happened in the past, everything that's happening now, and everything that will happen in the future. He knows how everything in the universe works and why everything happens. He knows every choice we'll ever face and the consequences of every option. He knows our true motives and deepest feelings. He knows how we can find ultimate fulfillment and happiness and how we can be most effective in serving Him. Paul said the highest levels of human thought are foolishness compared to God's wisdom (1 Corinthians 3:18–20).

God is sovereign. He has no boss and answers to no one. He is the ultimate authority on every subject. He's not obligated to do anything. He's not motivated by popularity or politics. He does what He wants when He wants. And everything He does is right and perfect simply because He does it.

God is transcendent. God is not contained by the universe or anything in it. He's distinct from His creation. He's not subject to the laws of physics or any other constraints in our world. He's also beyond the grasp of our intellect. If He hadn't taken the initiative in making Himself known, we would have no hope of understanding Him. In Isaiah 55:9, God explains His transcendence this way: "For as the heavens are higher than the earth, so are My ways higher than your ways and My thoughts than your thoughts."

God is unchanging. Numbers 23:19 says, "God is not a man, that He would lie, nor a son of man, that He would change His mind." James said that in God "there is no variation or shifting shadow" (James 1:17). Styles, standards, laws, and societies change. But God doesn't change, and neither do His promises. We can trust Him to be just who He says He is and do just what He says He will do. We can fully trust God not because of who we are and what we do but simply because of who God is.

DIG DEEP

The more time you spend in God's presence, studying His Word, speaking and listening to Him in prayer, the better you'll get to know Him. Ask yourself the following questions and answer them truthfully:

1. Do you fully trust God with every aspect of your life?
2. How does God's omniscience make it easier to trust Him?
3. Why is it comforting to know that God will never change?

Understanding God
Responding to Him

"But let the one who boasts boast of this, that he
understands and knows Me, that I am the LORD who
exercises mercy, justice, and righteousness on earth;
for I delight in these things," declares the LORD.
—JEREMIAH 9:24

GOD LOVINGLY AND GENEROUSLY REVEALS HIMSELF TO
us in His Word. Not only does He give us the privilege of learning
who He is, but He also gives us the opportunity to respond to Him
in a variety of ways.

First, *we can respond with wonder.* David asked in amazement,
"What is man that You think of him, and a son of man that You are
concerned for him?" (Psalm 8:4). We should never take for granted
our relationship with God. A part of us should always be overwhelmed by the privilege of calling God "Father."

Second, *we can respond with praise.* When we see a great play in a
rugby or a football match, we cheer. When we come face-to-face with
God's perfections, we respond with even more excitement. We show
our appreciation and awe for who He is and what He's done. We can
incorporate our praise in our worship for an even more powerful
experience.

Third, *we can respond with boldness.* Because of Jesus' sacrifice,
reborn believers don't have to cower in fear in God's presence.
Hebrews 4:16 says, "Therefore let's approach the throne of grace with
confidence, so that we may receive mercy and find grace for help

at the time of our need." We can take our requests to God without worrying about being tossed from His presence.

Fourth, *we can respond with purpose.* Look at the promise of John 14:13: "Whatever you ask in My name, this I will do." Imagine the possibilities when we pray and act within the will of God! God knows and sees all. He can do anything. He loves us and wants the very best for us. Think of the changes He can make in our lives, our families, our communities, and our world. He's ready, willing, and able to unleash His power and goodness for His purposes. God does not need anything or anyone, but He wants us to be His children and take part in His work.

Fifth, *we can respond with closeness.* James 4:8 says, "Come close to God and He will come close to you." We draw close to Him through prayer, Bible study, and following the example of His Son. He draws close to us by giving us His love, strength, support, encouragement, guidance, wisdom, discernment, peace, and fulfillment. He lives inside us through His Spirit, and through Him we can cry out, "Abba! Father!" (Romans 8:15).

Sixth, *we can respond with obedience.* If we truly love God, we will obey Him (John 14:15). If we truly believe that God knows everything, including the consequences of every possible action we might take, it only makes sense to rely on His guidance and follow His instructions for our lives.

--- **DIG DEEP** ---

When God revealed Himself to people in the Bible, such as Abraham and Moses, their lives were changed forever. Ask yourself the following questions and answer them truthfully:

1. How has your life been changed by God's revelation of Himself in His Word?
2. How can you draw closer to God?

Conclusion

IF THERE IS ONE CLEAR AND UNDENIABLE LESSON THAT we can learn from Jesus and the disciples who followed Him, it is to fully surrender to God's will at all times. We need to look closely at the lives of the apostles before and after they received the Holy Spirit. Each disciple learned to deny himself, pick up his cross, and follow Jesus. How did they learn this? From the Master, Jesus Christ Himself!

For three years the apostles followed Jesus, listened to His words, and saw what He did. Put yourself in their shoes and just think for a moment how much they could have learned from the words and actions of Jesus within this time period. But even though they had the perfect Teacher, they still made many mistakes.

LEARNING FROM OTHERS' MISTAKES

Let's take a look at Simon Peter:

- He rebuked Jesus (Matthew 16:22).
- He fell asleep three times when Jesus asked him to keep watch (Matthew 26:41).
- He even denied Jesus three times (Matthew 26:69–75).

Not only did Peter deny Jesus but he also argued when Jesus predicted he would deny Him. Throughout the Bible we see how godly men struggled and sinned against God time after time, but we can also learn a few things from their choices:

- No one is perfect and everyone sins sometimes.
- God understands that we will fall into sin.

- God corrects us when we sin.
- Even though God does not approve of our sins, He still loves us.
- God expects us to repent, learn from our failures, and continue on the road of sanctification.

What was Peter's problem? Why did he fail? He didn't deny his own self, and thus he denied Jesus. He wanted to serve Christ in his own way and it led only to sin. All the apostles had to learn to deny themselves and to follow Christ through the Spirit. After all, Jesus taught this important truth while He was with them, as recorded in Luke 9:23: "And He was saying to them all, 'If anyone wants to come after Me, he must deny himself, take up his cross daily, and follow Me.'"

LEARNING TO TRULY ABIDE IN CHRIST

My hope is that reading this ninety-day devotional has helped you realize this important truth: Jesus did not just die for you—you have to die with Him on the cross as well. Every reborn Christian needs to crucify himself, his own life, and his own will. And if he does not want to, he cannot call himself a reborn Christian.

God gave you a self to think on your own, a self-determining power by which you can choose what you want to do with your life. Why did God give this to you? Because He wants you to choose to obey out of free will, to bring yourself to Him every day on the road of sanctification, so He can bless you with His fullness and lead you forward in His will. He wants you to say, as Jesus did, "Not my will, but Yours be done" (Luke 22:42). This is the key to living a life of total victory, a life of complete surrender, and a life of unconditional peace.

If you want to experience this life, you need to say, "Father, fill my will, my cup, with Your perfect will, and let me become less so that You can become more within me." Paul also learned this incredible lesson when he said, "Therefore I delight in weaknesses, in insults, in distresses, in persecutions, in difficulties, in behalf of Christ; for when I am weak, then I am strong" (2 Corinthians 12:10).

If you have reached this phase of your spiritual growth, keep following Jesus as your example. Move forward and run the race with endurance until the end, just like the Bible reminds us in Hebrews 12:1–2.

> Therefore since we also have such a great cloud of witnesses surrounding us, let's rid ourselves of every obstacle and the sin which so easily entangles us, and let's run with endurance the race that is set before us, looking only at Jesus, the originator and perfecter of the faith, who for the joy set before Him endured the cross, despising the shame, and has sat down at the right hand of the throne of God.

Take these verses with you, write them on your heart, and continue to abide in Christ and share His truth with those around you. May the love and peace of Jesus Christ be with you wherever you go.

Three-Track Plan for Reading God's Word

OF ALL THE REASONS PEOPLE MENTION FOR NOT READ-ing the Bible, simple discouragement is the most common. The Bible's length alone is imposing. More like a self-contained library than a book, it includes sixty-six different books by several dozen authors. No wonder people get confused and discouraged.

The following three-track reading plan helps break these books of the Bible into more manageable portions. All three tracks share one thing in common: they each assign about one chapter a day, which should take only five to ten minutes to read.

If you're new to the Bible, begin with Track 1, then proceed to Track 2, and finally—if you're ambitious—tackle Track 3. Commit to one of these tracks today and let God do His work within you.

TRACK 1: INTRODUCTION TO THE NEW TESTAMENT

Time Commitment: One month
Goal: Survey New Testament biblical foundations

Track 1 is a great place to start reading the Bible. Two separate reading plans take you quickly into passages of the New Testament every Christian should know. These were selected with two concerns in mind: First, the passages are frequently quoted or referred to. Second, they are relatively easy to read and understand. Track 1 is a sampler designed to whet your appetite for more.

Two Weeks on the Life and Teachings of Jesus

- [ ] 1   **Luke 1:** Preparing for His arrival
- [ ] 2   **Luke 2:** Story of His birth
- [ ] 3   **Mark 1:** Beginning of Ministry
- [ ] 4   **Mark 9:** Day in the Life
- [ ] 5   **Matthew 5:** Sermon on the Mount
- [ ] 6   **Matthew 6:** Sermon on the Mount
- [ ] 7   **Luke 15:** Parables of Jesus
- [ ] 8   **John 3:** Conversation with Nicodemus
- [ ] 9   **John 14:** Final Instructions
- [ ] 10   **John 17:** Prayer for His Disciples
- [ ] 11   **Matthew 26:** Betrayal and Arrest
- [ ] 12   **Matthew 27:** Execution on a Cross
- [ ] 13   **John 20:** Resurrection
- [ ] 14   **Luke 24:** Appearances After the Resurrection

Two Weeks on the Life and Teachings of Paul

- [ ] 1   **Acts 9:** Conversion
- [ ] 2   **Acts 16:** Macedonian Call and Jailbreak
- [ ] 3   **Acts 17:** Missionary Journeys
- [ ] 4   **Acts 26:** Life Story
- [ ] 5   **Acts 27:** Shipwreck
- [ ] 6   **Acts 28:** Arrival in Rome
- [ ] 7   **Romans 3:** Theology Summary
- [ ] 8   **Romans 7:** Struggle with Sin
- [ ] 9   **Romans 8:** Life in the Spirit
- [ ] 10   **1 Corinthians 13:** Description of Love
- [ ] 11   **1 Corinthians 15:** Thoughts on the Afterlife
- [ ] 12   **Galatians 5:** Freedom in Christ
- [ ] 13   **Ephesians 3:** Summary of Mission
- [ ] 14   **Philippians 2:** Imitating Christ

TRACK 2: EVERY BOOK IN THE NEW TESTAMENT

Time Commitment: Three months
Goal: To gain an overview of the New Testament

Track 2 includes eighty-one New Testament chapters. Many well-known parts are not represented, and you will read only a single chapter from some books. But these sections have been selected because they are understandable without commentary to the average reader. Taken together, they provide a good foundation for understanding the New Testament.

Don't worry if you miss a few days. Just resume reading when you can. In about three months you will get an overview that includes a portion of every book in the New Testament.

Matthew

☐ 5   ☐ 6   ☐ 13   ☐ 19   ☐ 26   ☐ 27
☐ 28

Mark

☐ 1   ☐ 2   ☐ 3   ☐ 4   ☐ 5   ☐ 6
☐ 7   ☐ 8   ☐ 9   ☐ 10   ☐ 11   ☐ 12
☐ 13   ☐ 14   ☐ 15–16

Luke

☐ 1   ☐ 2   ☐ 10   ☐ 12   ☐ 15   ☐ 16
☐ 18   ☐ 24

John

☐ 3   ☐ 6   ☐ 10   ☐ 14   ☐ 15   ☐ 16
☐ 17   ☐ 20

Acts

☐ 1   ☐ 2   ☐ 5   ☐ 9   ☐ 16   ☐ 17
☐ 26   ☐ 27   ☐ 28

Romans

☐ 3   ☐ 7   ☐ 8   ☐ 12

1 Corinthians

☐ 13   ☐ 15

2 Corinthians

☐ 4   ☐ 12

Galatians

☐ 3

Ephesians

☐ 2   ☐ 3

Philippians

☐ 2

Colossians

☐ 1

1 Thessalonians

☐ 3   ☐ 4

2 Thessalonians

☐ 2

1 Timothy

☐ 1

2 Timothy

☐ 2

Titus

☐ 2

Philemon

☐ Philemon

Hebrews

☐ 2   ☐ 11   ☐ 12

James

☐ 1

1 Peter

☐ 1

2 Peter

☐ 1

1 John

☐ 3

2 John and 3 John

☐ 2 John and 3 John

Jude

☐ Jude

Revelation

☐ 1   ☐ 12   ☐ 21

TRACK 3: EVERY WORD OF THE NEW TESTAMENT, PSALMS, AND PROVERBS

Time Commitment: One year
Goal: To read all the way through the New Testament, Psalms, and Proverbs with understanding

Track 3 takes you completely through the New Testament, Psalms, and Proverbs, reading every word. This plan follows a relaxed pace, usually assigning only one chapter a day. (Some short chapters have been combined, so occasionally you will read two brief chapters in one day.) In all, the reading plan days work out evenly to a one-year total. This plan alternates between the New Testament and the books of Psalms and Proverbs, providing a nice variety for daily readings.

Matthew

☐ 1	☐ 2	☐ 3	☐ 4	☐ 5	☐ 6
☐ 7	☐ 8	☐ 9	☐ 10	☐ 11	☐ 12
☐ 13	☐ 14	☐ 15	☐ 16	☐ 17	☐ 18
☐ 19	☐ 20	☐ 21	☐ 22	☐ 23	☐ 24
☐ 25	☐ 26	☐ 27	☐ 28		

Psalms 1–10

☐ 1–2	☐ 3–4	☐ 5–6	☐ 7–8	☐ 9	☐ 10

Mark

☐ 1   ☐ 2   ☐ 3   ☐ 4   ☐ 5   ☐ 6
☐ 7   ☐ 8   ☐ 9   ☐ 10   ☐ 11   ☐ 12
☐ 13   ☐ 14   ☐ 15–16

Psalms 11–21

☐ 11–12   ☐ 13–14   ☐ 15–16   ☐ 17   ☐ 18   ☐ 19
☐ 20–21

Luke

☐ 1   ☐ 2   ☐ 3   ☐ 4   ☐ 5   ☐ 6
☐ 7   ☐ 8   ☐ 9   ☐ 10   ☐ 11   ☐ 12
☐ 13   ☐ 14   ☐ 15   ☐ 16   ☐ 17   ☐ 18
☐ 19   ☐ 20   ☐ 21   ☐ 22   ☐ 23   ☐ 24

Psalms 22–30

☐ 22   ☐ 23–24   ☐ 25   ☐ 26   ☐ 27–28   ☐ 29–30

John

☐ 1   ☐ 2   ☐ 3   ☐ 4   ☐ 5   ☐ 6
☐ 7   ☐ 8   ☐ 9   ☐ 10   ☐ 11   ☐ 12
☐ 13   ☐ 14   ☐ 15   ☐ 16   ☐ 17   ☐ 18
☐ 19   ☐ 20   ☐ 21

Psalms 31–40

☐ 31   ☐ 32   ☐ 33   ☐ 34   ☐ 35   ☐ 36
☐ 37   ☐ 38   ☐ 39   ☐ 40

Acts

☐ 1   ☐ 2   ☐ 3   ☐ 4   ☐ 5   ☐ 6
☐ 7   ☐ 8   ☐ 9   ☐ 10   ☐ 11   ☐ 12
☐ 13   ☐ 14   ☐ 15   ☐ 16   ☐ 17   ☐ 18
☐ 19   ☐ 20   ☐ 21   ☐ 22   ☐ 23   ☐ 24
☐ 25   ☐ 26   ☐ 27   ☐ 28

Psalms 41–50

☐ 41   ☐ 42–43   ☐ 44   ☐ 45–46   ☐ 47–48   ☐ 49
☐ 50

Romans

☐ 1   ☐ 2   ☐ 3   ☐ 4   ☐ 5   ☐ 6
☐ 7   ☐ 8   ☐ 9   ☐ 10   ☐ 11   ☐ 12–13
☐ 14   ☐ 15–16

Psalms 51–61

☐ 51   ☐ 52   ☐ 53–54   ☐ 55   ☐ 56–57   ☐ 58–59
☐ 60–61

1 Corinthians

☐ 1   ☐ 2–3   ☐ 4–5   ☐ 6   ☐ 7   ☐ 8–9
☐ 10   ☐ 11   ☐ 12   ☐ 13   ☐ 14   ☐ 15
☐ 16

Psalms 62–72

☐ 62–63   ☐ 64–65   ☐ 66–67   ☐ 68   ☐ 69   ☐ 70–71
☐ 72

2 Corinthians

☐ 1   ☐ 2–3   ☐ 4–5   ☐ 6–7   ☐ 8–9   ☐ 10
☐ 11   ☐ 12–13

Psalms 73–80

☐ 73   ☐ 74   ☐ 75–76   ☐ 77   ☐ 78   ☐ 79
☐ 80

Galatians

☐ 1   ☐ 2   ☐ 3   ☐ 4   ☐ 5–6

Psalms 81–90

☐ 81   ☐ 82–83   ☐ 84–85   ☐ 86–87   ☐ 88   ☐ 89
☐ 90

Ephesians

☐ 1   ☐ 2   ☐ 3   ☐ 4   ☐ 5   ☐ 6

Psalms 91–101

☐ 91   ☐ 92–93   ☐ 94–95   ☐ 96–97   ☐ 98–99   ☐ 100–101

Philippians

☐ 1   ☐ 2   ☐ 3   ☐ 4

Colossians

☐ 1   ☐ 2   ☐ 3

Psalms 102–111

☐ 102   ☐ 103   ☐ 104   ☐ 105   ☐ 106   ☐ 107
☐ 108   ☐ 109   ☐ 110–111

1 Thessalonians

☐ 1–2   ☐ 3–4   ☐ 5

2 Thessalonians

☐ 1–2   ☐ 3

Psalms 112–119

☐ 112–113   ☐ 114–115   ☐ 116–117
☐ 118   ☐ 119:1–48   ☐ 119:49–96
☐ 119:97–144   ☐ 119:145–176

1 Timothy

☐ 1–2   ☐ 3–4   ☐ 5   ☐ 6

2 Timothy

☐ 1   ☐ 2   ☐ 3–4

Psalms 120–130

☐ 120–121 ☐ 122–123 ☐ 124–125 ☐ 126–128 ☐ 129–130

Titus

☐ 1   ☐ 2–3

Philemon

☐ Philemon

Psalms 131–140

☐ 131–132 ☐ 133–134 ☐ 135   ☐ 136   ☐ 137–138 ☐ 139
☐ 140

Hebrews

☐ 1–2   ☐ 3–4   ☐ 5–6   ☐ 7   ☐ 8   ☐ 9
☐ 10   ☐ 11   ☐ 12   ☐ 13

Psalms 141–150

☐ 141–142 ☐ 143   ☐ 144   ☐ 145   ☐ 146   ☐ 147
☐ 148   ☐ 149–150

James

☐ 1   ☐ 2   ☐ 3–4   ☐ 5

Proverbs 1–10

☐ 1   ☐ 2   ☐ 3   ☐ 4   ☐ 5   ☐ 6
☐ 7   ☐ 8   ☐ 9   ☐ 10

1 Peter

☐ 1   ☐ 2   ☐ 3   ☐ 4–5

2 Peter

☐ 1   ☐ 2–3

Proverbs 11–20

☐ 11   ☐ 12   ☐ 13   ☐ 14   ☐ 15   ☐ 16
☐ 17   ☐ 18   ☐ 19   ☐ 20

1 John

☐ 1   ☐ 2   ☐ 3

2 and 3 John

☐ 2 John, 3 John

Jude

☐ Jude

Proverbs 21–31

☐ 21   ☐ 22   ☐ 23   ☐ 24   ☐ 25   ☐ 26
☐ 27   ☐ 28   ☐ 29   ☐ 30   ☐ 31

Revelation

☐ 1   ☐ 2   ☐ 3   ☐ 4–5   ☐ 6   ☐ 7–8
☐ 9   ☐ 10–11   ☐ 12   ☐ 13   ☐ 14   ☐ 15–16
☐ 17   ☐ 18   ☐ 19   ☐ 20   ☐ 21   ☐ 22

God's Promises When You . . .

Feel Guilty

> Psalm 130:3–4
> Romans 8:1–2
> 1 Corinthians 6:11
> Ephesians 3:12;
> Hebrews 10:22–23

Feel Dejected

> Psalm 130:7
> Isaiah 65:24
> Matthew 11:28–30
> Romans 8:26–27
> Hebrews 4:16
> James 4:8, 10

Feel Despair

> Psalm 119:116
> Isaiah 57:15
> Jeremiah 32:17
> Philippians 4:6–7

Are Disappointed

Psalm 22:4–5
Matthew 19:25–26
John 15:7
Romans 8:28
Ephesians 3:20
James 1:5–6

Are Depressed

Deuteronomy 31:8
Psalm 34:18
Isaiah 49:13–15
Romans 5:5

Are Persecuted

Psalm 37:1–2
Psalm 118:6
Matthew 5:10–12
2 Corinthians 4:8–12
2 Timothy 1:11–12;
1 Peter 3:13–14

Are Anxious

Psalm 55:22
Isaiah 41:13
Matthew 6:24–25
Matthew 11:28–29
Philippians 4:6–7
1 Peter 5:7

Are Filled With Longing

Psalm 37:4
Psalm 84:11
Proverbs 3:5–6
Luke 12:29–31

Are Sick

Psalm 23:4
Psalm 73:26
Proverbs 17:22
John 16:33
Romans 8:37–39
2 Corinthians 12:9–10
James 5:14–15

Are Impatient

Psalm 27:13–14
Psalm 37:7, 9
Romans 2:7
1 Timothy 1:16
Hebrews 6:12
2 Peter 3:9

Are Confused

Psalm 32:8
Isaiah 42:16
John 8:12
John 14:27
1 Corinthians 2:15–16
James 1:5

Are Tempted

Job 23:10–11
1 Corinthians 10:13
Hebrews 2:18
Hebrews 4:15–16
James 1:2–4, 13–14
1 Peter 5:8–10

Are Weak

Psalm 72:13
Isaiah 41:10
Romans 8:26
1 Corinthians 1:7–9
2 Corinthians 4:7–9
2 Corinthians 12:9–10

Are Afraid

Joshua 1:9
Psalm 4:8
Psalm 23:4
Romans 8:37–39
2 Corinthians 1:10
2 Timothy 1:7
Hebrews 13:6

Obey

Matthew 16:27
John 8:31–32
John 14:21, 23
Acts 5:29
James 1:25
James 2:26

Are in Need

Isaiah 58:11
John 6:35
Ephesians 3:20–21
Philippians 4:11–13, 19

Grieve

Psalm 119:50, 76–77
Jeremiah 31:13
Matthew 5:4
John 16:20–22
1 Thessalonians 4:13–14
Revelation 21:3–4

Suffer

Psalm 34:19
Nahum 1:7
John 16:33
Romans 8:16–17
1 Peter 2:20–21
1 Peter 4:12–13

Fail

Joshua 1:9
Romans 3:23–24
Romans 5:8
Hebrews 10:35–36
1 John 1:8–9

Doubt

Psalm 34:22
Matthew 14:28–33
John 3:18
James 1:5–8
Hebrews 11:1, 6

Acknowledgments

I WOULD LIKE TO GIVE A BIG AFRIKAANS "DANKIE" (thank you) to the team at the Steve Laube Agency where this project started. Special thanks to Dan Balow for guiding me through the whole process with patience and understanding.

Another huge dankie to Chris Hudson and Mary Larsen, who are part of the team from Peachtree Publishing Services, for their great communication and professionalism. All you guys are truly working hard to protect and advance God's Word.

A massive dankie to Randy Southern, my ghostwriter who worked extremely hard to help me rewrite my terrible Afrikaans-English words into "proper" English. This book would not have been possible without your help!

And a gigantic dankie to Daniel Marrs and Natalie Nyquist from Nelson Books and HarperCollins Christian Publishing, who diligently worked to make sure we have a devotional that sounds good, looks good, and is good. Your advice, guidance, and professionalism speak volumes for the talent that you have and use for God's glory! Daniel Marrs, few people can match your talent for effective communication with the limited amount of time that we had. Natalie Nyquist, thank you for the speedy communication and for helping me with the copyedit and the whole process. All of you definitely made the book a whole lot more readable than it would have been.

Nikita Maritz, my amazing wife, who always stepped up and took care of things for me when I was getting burned out. If it was not for her by my side, allowing me time, I would not have been able to write this devotional.

My amazing team at DLM Christian Lifestyle jumped in and took on more tasks so that I could make more time to work on this book. They are the unsung heroes who work incredibly hard behind the scenes to share the good news. Danie Ludeke, as their team manager, took a lot more on his plate so that I could have the time I needed to work on this project. He is an incredible worker, and God has been so gracious to me that I can call him my best friend. Caline van den Berg, who manages all my social media and double-checked my spelling at times when we struggled to find our feet, was also an incredible help! I am looking forward with excitement to seeing what God has planned for every member of DLM!

Ross and Liz Harris gave me a lot of advice and guidance through this process, which I appreciate immensely. They have also been with me every step of the way and triple-checked all the pages to make sure the book reads smoothly. I have grown very close to these two amazing people from Iowa.

Jay Hardy had been supporting me even before I started to work on this book and also gave me great advice over time. He has definitely been sent by God for this time in my life.

Lastly, all glory and honor go to God Himself, who continues to work in us and through us to change lives!

About the Author

DANIEL MARITZ IS A POPULAR YOUTUBER AND BIBLE teacher whose online ministries, DLM Christian Lifestyle and DLM Men's Lifestyle, reach hundreds of thousands across the globe with God's truth and love. Born in Namibia and raised in South Africa, Daniel is the youngest of five children and grew up in a loving home under the guidance of his preacher father. But it was not until tragedy—the death of his second brother—struck the family in Daniel's early twenties that he decided to truly accept Christ. Devoted to his calling from God to teach the fundamental truth of Scripture to all nations and all people, Daniel started to study theology through SATS (South African Theological Seminary). His aim is to bring people back to studying the Word of God and call all men and women to real discipleship by teaching them what it means to be a true, reborn Christian.